Making It Till Friday
A Guide to Successful Classroom Management

Dedicated to Lib, Blakeley, Gene, David, and Amy

MAKING IT TILL FRIDAY
A Guide to Successful Classroom Management

James D. Long
Appalachian State University

and

Virginia H. Frye
University of Tennessee

PRINCETON BOOK COMPANY, *Publishers*
Princeton, New Jersey

Sources of Cartoons

We gratefully acknowledge cartoonists
Ford Button (pages 23, 155, and 165), Walter Hagedorn
(page 39), Sidney Harris (page 121), and Henry R. Martin
(page 193) for permission to reprint their cartoons
which originally appeared in the *Phi Delta Kappan*;
and Jenny Gay for her original cartoon (page 71).

PREFACE

Today, perhaps more than in earlier times, widespread attention is being focused on problems in the schools. Numerous critics claim students are not learning fundamentals because teachers cannot control the students long enough to do any teaching. Some say the schools are veritable battlegrounds that are unsafe for both teachers and students. Almost every day, stories about assaults, chronic drug abuse, and racial unrest receive national news coverage. Although the problems of the schools often are overdramatized, myriad problems of varying degrees of difficulty confront every classroom teacher who is expected to solve those problems. Unfortunately, teachers are seldom taught to manage the situations confronting them because, too frequently, teacher training emphasizes educational and psychological principles without devoting sufficient attention to the practical use of those principles in the classroom. Some teachers have also been taught that *only* enthusiasm, hard work, love of others, or knowledge of the subject matter is needed to alleviate classroom difficulties. In either case, teachers are left without specific information needed for managing today's classes. Consequently, teachers tell their troubles to colleagues, worry a great deal, and hope they can survive until another weekend arrives.

The purpose of this book is to provide teachers and prospective teachers at all grade levels with practical suggestions for managing their classes more effectively. We do not presume to have all the answers. The solutions to problems such as racial hatred, drug abuse, and resentment toward those in authority may lie in basic societal changes. However, many problems that pervade the lives of teachers and students are amenable to solutions: seemingly unmotivated students can be helped to become interested in school. Aggressive students can learn to cooperate. Shy students can learn to interact appropriately. Certainly effective classroom management is not easy. Nonetheless, research studies have already uncovered solutions to many classroom management problems. This book will discuss many of those solutions along with practical procedures for using the findings of research in your classroom. We hope that as you read this book and undertake some of the suggested projects your life and the lives of your students will be enriched by your efforts.

We would like to thank those who have helped with the preparation of this book. We are grateful for the help of Don Clark, Joyce Crouch, Gene Frye, Dick Levin, Grace Lilly, Lib Long, Melver Padgett, Bob Williams, and Linda Vandiford. We also appreciate the suggestions of those teachers and students who have tested the ideas presented in the text and provided examples that appear throughout the book. All of these have done much to make our efforts more of a joy than a chore.

J.D.L.
V.H.F.

CONTENTS

vii

CHAPTER ONE

AN INTRODUCTION TO CLASSROOM MANAGEMENT

"Whew! I thought the day would never end. From the moment I entered that classroom this morning it has been one problem right after another. Billy and Darrell were at it the first thing. I had to send them both to the office for fighting. Suzie cried for over an hour because I scolded her for not having her math. And, to beat it all, I worked half the night planning a language arts lesson, and only a few of my better students seemed interested. To tell you the truth I don't know if I can make it till Friday."

"If you think you had a rough day, let me tell you what happened to me. You remember I was telling you about Johnny Johnson. Well, today he . . ."

And so the stories go in virtually every school. The misfortune, however, is not that teachers encounter problems. Every professional person does. The misfortune is that many teachers feel they lack the expertise to manage their classrooms effectively. Stephens and Evans (1973) suggest that as many as 70 percent of beginning teachers express concern about being able to manage students' behavior. Experienced teachers, too, express concern. Every year many intelligent, humane teachers leave the profession because of worries over classroom management.

Is There Cause For Alarm?

A great deal of justification can be found for concern about the prevalence of behavior problems in the schools. For instance, a report by the Department of Health, Education, and Welfare (1972) indicated that one child in five exhibited behavior that could be classified as excessive and a cause for concern. Others (e.g., Stennett, 1966; Swift, Spivack, Danset, Danset-Leger, and Winnykamen, 1972) have conducted studies that produced similar findings. Anyone who has ever taught in public schools can also attest that there is no shortage of problems. Indeed, behavior difficulties probably characterize all schools to some degree. While there is justification for concern about the presence of problems in the schools, the situation is far from hopeless. An abundance of strategies exists for helping teachers cope with the frustrations they encounter in teaching. A major purpose of this book is to present specific strategies for dealing with many of the current classroom problems. Of course, no guarantees can be offered for remedying *every* difficulty, but teachers who are willing to admit they have problems, examine the causes of the problems, and search for solutions should be able to resolve most of their difficulties. More teachers can learn to enjoy Mondays as much as (or almost as much as) Fridays.

Surprisingly, a few teachers give up too quickly. They let their honest concerns turn to despair. Recently, a young student teacher who had been working for two weeks in a first grade classroom remorsefully asked us, "Are there some students who just can't be helped?" Although we agreed that it might be possible, we questioned the advisability of giving up on a student, especially after such a brief period. Even children who engage primarily in undesirable behavior occasionally show appropriate behavior. One goal of effective classroom management is to recognize and systematically attempt to increase the child's positive behaviors, while minimizing the negative behaviors.

The Meaning of Classroom Management and Management Problems

A big step can be taken toward achieving effective classroom management by putting the issue into proper perspective. The term classroom management carries a number of different connotations. To some teachers it implies keeping order, to others, having students be polite, and to still others, the elimination of all undesirable student behaviors. These restricted notions tend to turn many teachers off to any discussion of classroom management. Most teachers would like to have more than a set of strategies that make their own jobs more pleasant. They want their efforts to enrich the lives of their students. They are desirous of teaching as much as they possibly can. In essence, the meaning of classroom management must reflect these desires of teachers.

Classroom management involves more than any single approach. It consists of numerous procedures for teaching a wide range of academic and social skills, and, certainly, it involves techniques that help teachers maintain order, instill desirable social skills, and weaken undesirable behaviors. But it is more, too. Classroom management includes all that teachers do to help students acquire useful skills, and the purpose is always to facilitate teaching—not merely to control or keep order. Thus, even when the focus is upon a limited aspect of management, such as weakening an undesirable behavior, the goal is to facilitate teaching other behaviors.

A classroom management problem can be any event or behavior that persistently interferes with the acquisition of desired social and academic skills. Management problems, then, actually represent problems in learning. Either the individual has failed to learn an appropriate behavior, has learned an inappropriate behavior, or has acquired the wrong amount of a behavior (too little or too much) for a given situation. This conception of the problem is considerably broader than the common interpretation, which emphasizes control of undesirable or excessive amounts of behaviors. Of course, classroom management entails setting upper limits on behavior, but a teacher would be wise to consider setting lower limits, too. If an individual consistently fails to interact with others, withdraws, or fails to turn in the assigned written material, does he not present a problem? While such behaviors may not cause nearly the disruption created by acting out behaviors, they can constitute extremely oppositional behavior, and they do present problems in learning. Thus, effective classroom management entails the production of desirable behaviors as well as the elimination of undesirable behaviors. In fact, many undesirable behaviors may not be exhibited if teachers can produce appropriate academic and social behaviors.

When the purpose of classroom management is viewed as promoting instruction, and the definition of a management problem is seen as a problem in learning, teachers may be expected to ask, "What is the best way I can help this student learn what he needs to learn?" Undoubtedly, teachers will also be less inclined to make accusations, look for ways to punish, or just feel sorry about the situation they are in. Similarly, students who present problems are more likely to be perceived as needing assistance than as trouble makers. The way teachers look at problems, then, has a great deal to do with how they attempt to solve them.

Characteristics of Effective Classroom Management

A variety of teaching styles and behaviors are used in today's classroom. Nonetheless, several principal characteristics do seem to be present in all classes that have high productivity and high morale. These characteristics are: (1) a concern for students, (2) an emphasis on positive, rather than punitive strategies, and (3) an active involvement of students in classroom management.

Concern for Students

While no one can establish the absolute impact of a teacher's concern for students, it seems certain that effective classroom management cannot exist without a genuine concern for students. Students may refer to concern as interest, respect, helpfulness, friendliness, fairness, or by a host of other names. The result is always the same; students behave differently when they feel the teacher is interested in them. They share their ideas, worries, hopes, fears, and desires with the teacher who cares. The teacher is thus in a better position really to help the students. A teacher needs only to recall his or her own experiences as a student to verify the positive behavior changes that result from coming in contact with an adult who is concerned about others. The work of prominent psychologists (e.g., Combs, 1974; Rogers, 1969) also substantiates that teaching and learning are enhanced when the teacher exhibits concern for students.

A big question for teachers, then, is, "How do I determine the extent of my concern for students?" This question is important because teachers are likely to produce meaningful changes in themselves only when they are aware of their own feelings and behaviors. Generally, concern is reflected in all the attitudes (and more precisely in the specific behaviors making up these attitudes) that teachers display towards others. Since attitudes are dealt with in detail later in this book, one needs only to recognize at this point that teachers' concern for students is an essential aspect of effective classroom management.

An Emphasis on Positive Strategies

Teachers who are effective in managing classrooms rely more heavily on positive than on punitive strategies. Positive strategies consist of actions that increase desirable behaviors. Encouragement, recognition, and praise are some examples. Conversely, punitive strategies are intended to suppress unwanted behaviors. Corporal punishment, sarcasm, criticism, and frowns are examples. Enter a class where positive strategies predominate, and you are likely to see a happy, productive group. Enter a class where the teacher fusses a great deal, berates the students, and in general relies upon punishment, and you are apt to see misbehavior. Kounin and Gump (1961) found that more misbehavior (e.g., aggression, inattention, lack of concern for academics) occurs in classes conducted by punitive teachers than in those conducted by nonpunitive teachers. Other researchers (Madsen, Becker, Thomas, Koser, and Plager, 1968; Thomas, Becker, and Armstrong, 1968) have demonstrated that teachers can actually create a disruptive class by systematically increasing the amount of disapproval given to students. Still other studies (Kazdin and Klock, 1973; Becker, Madsen, Arnold and Thomas, 1967; McAllister, Stachowiak, Baer, and Conderman, 1969) have shown that increased use of positive strategies (e.g., verbal and nonverbal approval) can reduce problem behaviors. A general conclusion is that the teachers who rely primarily on positive strategies are also the teachers who are most effective in managing their classrooms.

Given time, skillful teachers probably discover that problems can be prevented and unwanted behaviors substantially reduced by strengthening what students do correctly. Occasionally, however, a teacher may come to believe that punitive measures alone will produce an efficient classroom. Admittedly, some teachers can instill enough fear in students to maintain silence and a semblance of productivity, but this approach cannot be construed as effective management. Effective management exists when students are free of threat so that optimal opportunities for learning prevail. An excessively punitive atmosphere will subdue a lot of appropriate as well as inappropriate behaviors. In addition, undesirable side effects may accompany the application of punishment, especially corporal punishment. Students may turn away from school, the teacher, and any other events closely associated with the punishment. Paradoxically, the dispenser of punishment can also serve as an aggressive model for students to imitate. The legal difficulties that can ensue from unwise use of corporal punishment can also add to the teacher's problems. Failure to seek alternative behavior change techniques may embroil teachers in bitter disputes with students and parents.

Although positive intervention is the technique of choice for most classroom situations, there are times when effective behavior management may appropriately involve some negative intervention. For example, when a student engages in repeated episodes of misconduct, or exhibits behaviors that may jeopardize the safety of other students, a rapid suppression of the undesirable behavior may be necessary. Even for these behaviors, the intervention does not have to be the application of aversive stimuli. Techniques, such as the temporary removal of the student from a troublesome situation (time out) or the temporary removal of rewards (response cost), can be used to reduce inappropriate behaviors without the likelihood of side effects from delivering an aversive stimulus (as with punitive measures such as corporal punishment). Nonetheless, classes *characterized* by frequent use of any punitive strategies are not well managed. Our point here is only that classroom management may appropriately involve *some* negative intervention. Positive strategies should still predominate, however.

Involving Students in Classroom Management

A third factor that seems to characterize effectively managed classrooms is the active involvement of students in decision-making processes. An experimental study (Arwood, Williams, and Long, 1974) in a ninth grade English class exemplifies the benefits of student involvement. In one phase of that study, the teacher precisely defined what was considered to be appropriate and inappropriate behaviors and specified what would be the consequences (rewards and punishments) for each type of behavior. The students were left out of the planning. Under the clearly specified conditions provided by the teacher, the students made improvements in their social conduct. They talked less during the teacher's lectures, appeared to be more attentive, sat straighter, and threw fewer spitwads. But they did not improve academically. Only when they were involved in the planning did they improve both socially and academically. The researchers hypothesized that when these students were excluded from decision-making processes, they simply went through the motions to earn rewards. A commitment to perform well—not just look busy—may well come only when students feel they have some control over their own destinies.

Other studies with special education students (Long and Williams, 1976; Lovitt and Curtiss, 1969), elementary students (Bolstad and Johnson, 1972; Glynn, Thomas, and Shee, 1973), and junior high and senior high school students (Glynn, 1970; Williams, Long and Yoakley, 1972) suggest that student involvement holds considerable promise for improving academic and social behaviors. Indeed, it seems doubtful that effective classroom management can exist when a teacher assumes total responsibility for it. Students need to learn that they have some responsibility for behaving appropriately. They are the ones who need to learn the academic and social skills. The role of the teacher should not be to stand over students and make them behave. Under such conditions, students may never learn to manage their own behaviors. School thus becomes less meaningful for everyone.

While most teachers will agree that involvement of students can provide motivation to learn and can enhance enjoyment of school, the idea of student involvement raises an important question. How can teachers offer the freedom for students to participate in classroom management without creating havoc in the routine? The answer would seem to be that students must *earn* the right to participate in managing the classroom. Teachers can begin by gradually decreasing the amount of control they exert. As students demonstrate successes, the number of choices and the amount of freedom given can be increased. Teachers can not hope to manage a classroom effectively as long as they single-handedly assume responsibility for all decisions. Effective teaching occurs only to the extent that others learn to control themselves. After all, self-responsibility is a primary goal of all educational endeavors.

The Teacher's Responsibilities

Much of what has been said thus far suggests that the teacher has a major responsibility for helping youngsters learn those skills that will lead to an enriched life. Even when students are learning self-control, the teacher has a responsibility for arranging classroom conditions so that students can develop to their fullest potentials. Unfortunately, school personnel do not always realize the extent of their own responsibilities. The home, the peer group, and the community are too frequently held responsible for problems that are amenable to change within the classroom. In a recent survey of classroom problems among public school administrators (Long, 1976), the administrators saw the teacher or the school as being partially responsible for less than 10 percent of the reported problems. An unfavorable home background was listed as a source of problems ranging from being impolite to the teacher and tearing down a bulletin board to fighting on the school bus and disrupting academic activities. The students, the community, and the home were cited as being responsible for about 90 percent of the more than 240 classroom problems reported by the administrators. An earlier study (Barnes, 1963) among elementary teachers also found that factors related to the home were most often believed to contribute to classroom problems.

Certainly, most people would agree that a student's home life, his neighborhood, or his friends contribute to his behavior in the classroom. However, when teachers and principals make this point, they must realize that the school, too, is a part of every student's environment. Accepting one's own influence, or potential to influence, would then seem to be a fundamental prerequisite to producing lasting changes. If a child lacks an interest in the school, can the school do anything to remedy that circumstance? Little can be achieved by attributing all problem situations to the home, the community, or the students. A willingness to accept responsibility for helping youngsters learn new and alternative ways of behaving can result in a more productive approach. Teachers and school administrators who can accept responsibility for producing change are on the way to establishing effective classroom management.

What Lies Ahead

Now that you have a brief description of classroom management, you may be wondering what lies ahead in the remaining chapters. In other words, how can this book help you? Will it, for example, provide techniques that are appropriate for secondary as well as elementary teachers? We definitely think so. Sometimes a technique that is appropriate for one age group may be inappropriate for another. Where a technique is more appropriate for one group than another, we will tell you. Often it is only the way in which a technique is applied that is different. In any event, each of the remaining chapters will in some way focus on helping teachers at every grade level to establish effective classroom management. That is, information will be oriented towards helping teachers demonstrate concern for students, develop alternatives to the use of aversive control, and involve students in developing greater self-control. A brief description of what each chapter is intended to convey is presented below.

Format of the Remaining Chapters

Chapter Two emphasizes how teacher attitudes towards self and others can influence classroom management. By taking a closer look at themselves, teachers should be in a better position to prevent many classroom management problems as well as to cope with existing ones. Chapter Three identifies strategies that can be used to cue appropriate behavior and thus reduce the need for reliance on punitive tactics. One key to classroom management lies not so much in how a teacher responds to problems after they have occurred, as in what is done to prevent the problems from occurring in the first place. Chapter Four identifies those strategies that can be used to maintain desirable responses once they have occurred. In addition, strategies for managing the overlooked problems of too little desirable behavior are explored. This chapter recognizes that students do not have to be disruptive to present problems for themselves and others. In fact, shy and withdrawn students may sometimes represent more serious problems than students who are loud and boisterous. Chapter Five recognizes that all problems cannot be prevented and that strategies are needed for dealing with excessively disruptive behaviors. Teachers should find this chapter helpful in identifying ways for establishing order in a classroom. Chapter Six offers suggestions for working with parents, principals, school counselors, school psychologists, and others in achieving effective classroom management. Chapter Seven stresses that day-to-day classroom affairs should be governed by the long-range goal of all education, which is for students to attain self-responsibility. Chapter Eight discusses the ethical issues involved in classroom management and the necessity for recognizing basic student rights. No teacher or prospective teacher should overlook the legal and personal dilemma that can result from using unsound management procedures. Finally, the last chapter of the book demonstrates how materials in the preceding chapters can be combined to alleviate specific behavior problems. You will also find projects in each chapter that should help sharpen your classroom management skills.

REFERENCES

Arwood, B.; Williams, R. L.; and Long, J. D. "The effects of behavior contracts and behavior proclamations on social conduct and academic achievement in a ninth grade English class." *Adolescence* 9 (1974): 425–36.

Barnes, D. L. "An analysis of remedial activities used by elementary teachers in coping with classroom behavior problems." *The Journal of Educational Research* (1963): 544–47.

Becker, W. C.; Madsen, C. H., Jr.; Arnold, C. R.; and Thomas, D. R. "The contingent use of teacher attention and praise in reducing classroom behavior problems." *Journal of Special Education* 1 (1967): 287–307.

Bolstad, O. D., and Johnson, S. M. "Self-regulation in the modification of disruptive behavior." *Journal of Applied Behavior Analysis* 5 (1972): 443–54.

Combs, A. W. et al. *The professional education of teachers*, 2nd ed. Boston: Allyn and Bacon, Inc., 1974.

Glynn, E. L. "Classroom applications of self-determined reinforcement." *Journal of Applied Behavior Analysis* 3 (1970): 123–32.

Glynn, E. L.; Thomas, J. D.; and Shee, S. M. "Behavioral self-control of on-task behavior in an elementary classroom." *Journal of Applied Behavior Analysis* 6 (1973): 105–13.

Kazdin, A. E., and Klock, J. "The effects of nonverbal teacher approval on student attentive behavior." *Journal of Applied Behavior Analysis* 6 (1973): 643–54.

Kounin, J. S., and Gump, P. V. "The comparative influence of punitive and nonpunitive teachers upon children's concepts of school misconduct." *Journal of Educational Psychology* 52 (1961): 44–49.

Long, J. D. "A survey of the presumed causes and administrative actions taken for school disciplinary problems." Unpublished manuscript. Appalachian State University, 1976.

Long, J. D., and Williams, R. L. "The utility of self-management strategies in altering the classroom behaviors of mentally retarded adolescents." *Adolescence* 11 (1976): 29–38.

Lovitt, T. C., and Curtiss, K. "Academic response rate as a function of teacher- and self-imposed contingencies." *Journal of Applied Behavior Analysis* 2 (1969): 49–53.

Madsen, C. H., Jr.; Becker, W. C.; Thomas, D. R.; Koser, L.; and Plazer, E. "An analysis of the reinforcing function of 'sit down' commands." In R. K. Parker (Ed.), *Readings in educational psychology.* Boston: Allyn and Bacon, Inc., 1968.

McAllister, L. W.; Stachowiak, J. G.; Baer, D. M.; and Conderman, L. "The application of operant conditioning techniques in a secondary school classroom." *Journal of Applied Behavior Analysis* 2 (1969): 277–85.

Rogers, C. R. *Freedom to learn.* Columbus, Ohio: Charles E. Merrill, 1969.

Stennett, R. G. "Emotional handicap in the elementary years: Phase or disease?" *American Journal of Orthopsychiatry* 36 (1966): 444–49.

Stephens, J. M., and Evans, E. D. *Development and classroom learning: An introduction to educational psychology.* New York: Holt, Rinehart and Winston, 1973.

Swift, M. S.: Spivack, G.; Danset, A.; Danset-Leger, J.; and Winnykamen, F. "Classroom behavior and academic success of French and American elementary school children." *International Review of Applied Psychology* 20 (1972): 1–11.

Thomas, D. R.; Becker, W. C.; and Armstrong, M. "Production and elimination of disruptive classroom behavior by systematically varying teachers' behavior." *Journal of Applied Behavior Analysis* 1 (1968): 35–45.

United States Department of Health, Education, and Welfare, Public Health Services. *Behavior Patterns of Children in School. Vital Health Statistics* 11 (1972): 1–78.

Williams, R. L.; Long, J. D.; and Yoakley, R. W. "The utility of behavior contracts and behavior proclamations with advantaged senior high school students." *Journal of School Psychology* 10 (1972): 329-38.

CHAPTER TWO

THE EYE OF THE BEHOLDER

As we indicated in Chapter One, changing student behavior is not the only productive route to effective classroom management. The teacher represents an important variable in every classroom. What the teacher says and does has important influences on students' behavior. A teacher's perception of a behavioral incident can also have a profound effect on subsequent events in the classroom. An incident that is viewed as trivial by one teacher may reach catastrophic proportions for another. Thus, a teacher's behavior may be altered by the way classroom events are perceived and may result in a consequent effect on student behavior. Sometimes the way a teacher looks at a situation constitutes the actual problem.

Why is a particular behavior perceived differently by different people? How can one teacher remain objective about a situation, while another loses all objectivity in the same situation? It is primarily because the past experiences of each teacher have been different. Each teacher enters the classroom with attitudes that are well entrenched and that result in a predisposition to react to a particular classroom situation in a given manner. Only by examining personal attitudes that may affect perception of a behavioral incident can a teacher determine whether the behavior of a student actually needs changing.

The emphasis in this chapter is on teacher attitudes toward self and others, how these attitudes may affect behavior, and strategies for self-change. The discussion of teacher attitudes should not be interpreted as a personal indictment. Quite the contrary. Teachers who willingly examine all aspects of a problem can expect to make increased progress in achieving a positive classroom atmosphere.

Behaviors Reflect Feelings

Each individual has many attitudes—about self, work, education, and other people. Each attitude is composed of specific thoughts, feelings, and overt behaviors that reflect how the individual actually feels. An attitude toward others, for example, is made up of the thoughts, feelings, and behaviors exhibited by the individual toward others. An attitude about self may consist of entirely different thoughts, feelings, and behaviors. Later in the chapter, when we talk about changing attitudes, it will be seen that in order to change an attitude it is necessary to change the components that make up the attitude.

Only the individual can be cognizant of personal feelings. Nonetheless, others can, and do, draw inferences from the things the individual says and does. Words, gestures, tones, inflections, glances, and innumerable other verbal and nonverbal behaviors convey significant information about feelings. Students quickly determine whether teachers feel positively or negatively toward them, whether teachers are sure or unsure of themselves, whether teachers do or do not like their work, and so on. The inferences that students draw about teacher attitudes have a profound influence on interpersonal relationships in the classroom.

Unfortunately, many teachers get caught up in daily activities and never really think about their own attitudes. Teaching can be hectic. But sooner or later teachers should take time to consider their attitudes. Why not begin by examining two of the most crucial variables involved in teaching: attitudes toward others and attitudes toward self?

Attitudes Toward Others

The potential for influencing student behavior obviously can be increased or diminished by one's attitudes toward students. Indeed, some psychologists believe that teacher attitudes are *the* major factors that determine what students learn. Carl Rogers, for example, contends that certain teacher attitudes can serve to free students to raise questions, seek answers, and become self-directive. He says:

> ...such learning rests not upon the teaching skills of the teacher, not upon his scholarly knowledge of the field, not upon his curricular planning, not upon his use of audio-visual aids, not upon the

programmed learning he utilizes, not upon his lectures and presentations, not upon an abundance of books, though each of these might at one time or another be utilized as an important resource. No, the facilitation of significant learning rests upon certain attitudinal qualities which exist in the personal relationship between the facilitator and the learner.[1] (pp. 105-6)

Three Important Attitudes

Although you may not agree completely with Rogers, you may be wondering what these attitudes are that he deems so important to the facilitation of learning. Rogers has identified three teacher attitudes that he believes are necessary and sufficient conditions for establishing effective relationships and for the facilitation of learning. These are: (1) realness or genuineness, (2) prizing, acceptance, trust and (3) empathic understanding. Let us examine each of these in more detail.

Realness, Genuineness. Rogers describes real or genuine teachers as persons who,under appropriate conditions, are aware of their feelings. Such persons do not try to put up a facade or pretend to feel differently than they do. In other words, the attitude of realness involves being honest with oneself and with others.

Perhaps a classroom example will further clarify the meaning of realness. A fifth grade teacher recently related the following story to us. She explained that she had extremely negative feelings toward one of her students. Possibly she spent less time with that student, called on her less often, or was quick to criticize her. In any event, the student picked up the teacher's feelings and finally asked, "Do you like me?" The teacher was really surprised by this question. Instead of being dishonest, something that would have been apparent anyhow, the teacher admitted, "I have been upset by certain of your behaviors." This honest admission led to a discussion of what was bothering the teacher and ultimately to a new, friendlier relationship between the teacher and the student.

Although realness means that teachers may occasionally admit being angry, happy, sad, bored, or excited, it is not a license to go around putting others down. Realness means that teachers focus

[1]C. R. Rogers, *Freedom to Learn* (Columbus, Ohio: Charles E. Merrill Publishing Company, 1969).

on their *own* feelings. They don't disguise how they feel by blaming others. For example, the honest teacher is more apt to say "*I am upset by this arrangement*" than "*You* students don't know how to get organized." Realness, then, means that individuals recognize personal feelings as their *own* —not someone else's.

If you are beginning to question the idea of being honest about your feelings, you might want to consider the alternatives. How many teachers do you know who try to hide their feelings, only to have those feelings come out in the form of sarcasm and fault-finding? In deciding whether it would be appropriate to express your feelings, you might ask; "What will be the result to myself and to others if I do not express how I feel?"

Prizing, Acceptance, Trust.   For Rogers, the attitudes of prizing, acceptance, and trust mean that the teacher values the student's feelings, opinions, and person. These attitudes reflect a kind of unconditional positive regard in which the student need not be academic, handsome, or even well–behaved in order to be appreciated. Teachers who possess the attitude of acceptance see each individual as being a person of worth. Teachers with this attitude also appreciate individual differences among students. They accept occasional apathy, differences of opinion, and lack of conformity. Rogers says that accepting teachers realize they are dealing with imperfect human beings possessing many feelings and potentials.

Acceptance should not be interpreted as meaning that one must tolerate every student behavior. Teachers would be dishonest to pretend they could accept every student act. Furthermore, students would have no standards to follow if everything they did were condoned. Teachers can tell students that certain behavior is unacceptable without rejecting them. Saying, "Bill, please don't interrupt" is quite different from exclaiming, "Bill, you don't have any manners!" The first comment is directed at behavior; the second comment implies that something is wrong with the person. We can find no justification for rejecting a student as a person. When one does so, the attitudes of prizing and accepting the student are lost. Rejecting a behavior, however, is a different matter. But even with behavior, too much rejection can show a great deal about how the student is being perceived.

Empathic Understanding.   Rogers describes empathic understanding as sensitive awareness of the way education and learning appear to the student. It means the teacher actually experiences the way the student is feeling. The empathic teacher stands inside the other's shoes, so to speak, and views the world from that person's position. Thus, empathy enables the teacher to communicate an accurate understanding of what the other person is feeling.

The empathic teacher stands in sharp contrast to the one who is unable to accept honest emotional expressions from the students. The latter may comment, "I am surprised at you" or "Don't you dare say that again." Such statements tend to cut off communication. The empathic teacher increases communication by responding to the feelings behind a student's words or actions. For example, he may comment, "Sue, you feel like you may have been mistreated," "Bill, you seem upset by the discussion," "Joe, you act as though you would rather be working on another project," or "John, you seem very concerned about your performance." These and similar statements increase open communications, correct errors in teacher comprehension, and help students recognize what they are communicating to others. Students who recognize what they are feeling may desire to change. If feelings are never brought out in the open, they may never have the opportunity for complete self-awareness. Remember, however, *the empathic teacher is trying to communicate an understanding of student feelings, not to judge, evaluate, justify behavior, or prohibit expression of emotions.*

A Note of Clarification. The attitudes discussed above are sometimes very difficult to display. It is questionable whether anyone can ever be completely genuine, accepting, and empathic. The behavior of some students alone can make it difficult, if not impossible, for a teacher to exhibit the desired attitudes. Furthermore, Rogers himself recognizes that these qualities are rarely attained. Nonetheless, the ability to have a favorable and long lasting influence on others will be enhanced to the extent that a teacher is able to be genuine, accepting, and empathic. Similarly, students who are accepted without reservations have no need to defend themselves. They can explore other possibilities. As their feelings are understood, they may come to be more understanding of the feelings of others. Improvements in attitudes can make a significant change in one's own life and in the lives of others.

Assessing Your Attitudes Toward Others
    After reading about genuine, accepting, and empathic

teachers, you may be wondering what attitudes you really exhibit toward others. You may be having doubts about how honest, accepting, or empathic you are or you may be wondering how friendly, consistent, or fair you have been with others. One way to find out about your attitudes is to conduct a self-examination. You might begin by answering the questions given below. Of course, you will want to add others as you proceed with your self-examination.

_____ Are you afraid to tell others how you really feel?
_____ Do you feel comfortable about disagreeing with others?
_____ Are you afraid to tell others about yourself for fear they may dislike you?
_____ Do you believe others are basically trustworthy?
_____ Are you reluctant to involve students in planning classroom activities?
_____ Do you usually find something of value in every person or do you value only persons who exhibit certain kinds of behavior?
_____ Are students free to disagree with you?
_____ Do you try to understand the feelings which are associated with what others say and do?
_____ Can students (or others) approach you with any kind of problem?

You may know the answers to a few or all of the above questions. The answers to others may require more effort. You may need to carry a note pad for a few days and record your behaviors toward others. Or, you may wish to have someone else keep a record of how you act. In the next chapter, we will discuss a simplified record keeping system that can be used in analyzing your interactions with others. Regardless of what methods you select, an occasional reexamination of your attitudes should help you in initiating and evaluating behavior changes.

Strategies for Change

Once you have completed your self-examination, you may be desirous of implementing changes in your attitudes toward others. Some suggestions for making these changes are listed below. Our list is not inclusive, however. Our intention is primarily to help you get started changing some of the specific behaviors that go into making up a variety of positive attitudes toward others. By changing enough of the behaviors that comprise attitudes, you eventually change these attitudes. You may need to add to your list as you think of other behaviors related to the attitudes you are most interested in changing.

Be Willing to Admit Mistakes. Perhaps nothing is more reflective of genuineness than being willing to admit some human frailties. Admitting mistakes is not easy, though. A mystique seems to have grown up around teachers. Many persons act as though teachers are supposed to be paragons of virtue. Given this assumption, you could have a difficult time saying, "I was in error," "I goofed," "You are right," or "Please accept my apology." People who can never be wrong may be faced with the problem of having to distort circumstances so as to place themselves in a positive light. Those who can admit mistakes have no need to distort reality. They can see themselves and others in clearer perspective. Furthermore, teachers who can admit weaknesses are more likely to make it easy for students to admit mistakes and seek ways of improving. Shortcomings should not be a primary focus, but one should be able to accept one's own humanness. The realization that one has weaknesses may be prerequisite to actually admitting mistakes.

Listen to Others. Listening can be an especially helpful procedure for changing attitudes toward others because it permits one to learn more about what others really think and feel. Listening also communicates to others that one is interested in them and what they have to say. Thus, others are more likely to be receptive. Unfortunately, most of us do more talking than listening. Bellack and others (1966), for instance, concluded from their studies of interactions between teachers and students that teachers account for 70 percent of all talking in a class. Adams and Biddle (1970) found that teachers were the center of attention in over 80 percent of class conversations. Having a captive audience probably has a lot to do with the amount of talking teachers do. Naturally, teachers can never hope to learn about others by doing all the talking.

To improve your own listening ability, you might want to record the amount of time you spend talking and listening to others. A stopwatch could be used for documentation. Our college students who have done this have generally been surprised by the amount of talking they do. If you should try the strategy and obtain similar results, you might enlist the aid of a friend to give cues when you should be listening. A friend could also provide feedback on the quality of your listening.

Obviously, listening to others involves more than passive toleration of what others are saying. Paraphrasing and commenting directly on what others have said, for example, let others know that you are actually listening. Paraphrasing also permits clarification of any misunderstanding on your part. A good way to begin a paraphrase is to comment, "You think..." or "You are suggesting..." or "You recommend..." Paraphrasing, however, should be more than a mere parroting of what others have said. Effective listeners communicate that they have heard more than words. When you discern that others are happy, sad, frustrated, angry, and so on, this understanding should be communicated. An appropriate comment might be, "You feel let down by..." "You can't make up your mind about..." "You are strongly in favor of..." Listening, then, means that the listener is tuned in to the verbal and nonverbal expressions of others. And by being tuned in, much is learned about the needs, desires, hopes, and frustrations of other persons. Such knowledge is a step in changing attitudes. Often the more one learns about other people the more others are appreciated.

How much listening are you doing? Do you put aside what you are doing when others want to talk? Do you avoid interrupting others? Do you comment on what others say or do you switch conversations to what you want to talk about? Are you attentive to the feelings that words and nonverval behaviors convey? Do you really hear what others are saying or do you spend your listening time thinking of what you wish to say next?

Look for Positive Qualities in Others. Occasionally, a teacher may become aware of knowing only bad things about certain students. Such a situation may arise when he is confronted with highly disruptive students, who often appear to be more disorderly than they actually are. It is not uncommon to hear teachers say, "He never does *anything* right." No student is totally bad, however. Even the most disruptive students usually exhibit 25 to 50 percent appropriate behavior (Williams and Anandam, 1973). The commendable qualities that exist in every person must be recognized. Otherwise, one may never be able to develop positive attitudes toward some individuals.

To help focus on the positive qualities in others, you might try talking informally with your students. Desirable times for talking may be during lunch hours, before or after school, or at school social functions. These settings offer unique opportunities for getting to know more about students' interests, special talents, and needs. We frequently find that informal conversations give us much more positive attitudes toward students than can be acquired through classroom discussions alone. But we do have a word of caution. A few students may reject initial efforts to get to know them better. More than one try is often needed to convince these students of your interests in them. Teachers who take the time to talk with students will usually find that they have positive qualities that may have been overlooked in the classroom.

Respond More Positively to Others.   At least a part of our attitudes toward others is a function of how others respond to us. Research in classroom settings (Graubard, Rosenburg, and Miller, 1971; Klein, 1971; Sherman and Cormier, 1974) has shown that student behavior has a predictable influence on teacher behavior. The evidence from these studies indicates that when students behave appropriately (e.g., are attentive, follow directions), the teacher is more positive (e.g., praising). Conversely, when students are disruptive of learning activities, the teacher is more critical and reprimanding. You may realize from your own school experiences how students can affect the teacher. We certainly can. We have seen teachers in tears run from the classroom because of things the students said and did. It is very difficult for anyone to enjoy teaching and to have positive attitudes toward students who are responding negatively.

An important question, then, is how to get students to respond positively toward you. The answer seems to lie in deliberately increasing positive responses to the students. The principle of reciprocal liking appears to exist in most human relationships. That is, others like us to about the extent that we like them. Students respond more positively when responses to them have been positive.

Put Misbehavior in Perspective.   Much of students' misbehavior is unrelated to their real feelings about the teacher. Problems at home or with peers, disappointments over a performance, or any number of frustrations could lead students to misbehave. Even when a student openly expresses a dislike for the teacher, it may be the position the teacher holds—not the teacher—that is disliked. Teachers must therefore avoid taking misbehavior as a personal affront. A more productive approach, in terms of increasing favorable student and teacher attitudes in the classroom, involves viewing the misbehavior as a problem that can be remedied, and developing a behavior–change strategy. Establishing a dialogue with the offending students and observing their behavior may reveal the sources of the problem and suggest possible solutions. By putting the behavior of students in an objective perspective, you increase the likelihood of responding more positively to the students.

Seek Feedback from Others. Obtaining feedback from others can be helpful in gaining greater understanding of personal attitudes as well as in helping change those attitudes. A great deal of informative feedback can be obtained just by listening to what others have to say. College professors, principals, and supervisors may make periodic comments, and friends may also mention your behavior in their conversations with you. Students are another source of valuable information. Too often, however, we do not listen to what others say. We may interrupt when they try to emphasize a positive quality. "Oh, you don't really know me," we say. Or, we become argumentative when someone tries to give helpful criticism. Obviously, tuning out what others have to say negates understanding more about oneself. Taking the opportunity to listen can provide a means for identifying needed changes in attitudes and may also be helpful in changing attitudes.

If listening by itself proves inadequate, you may want to ask others for their opinions. If you do ask for feedback, we have a few suggestions that may prove useful. First, in soliciting feedback, one should be as precise as possible. Suppose you ask a friend to help you judge your attitudes toward others. Is your friend supposed to concentrate on the number of times you listen to others, your enthusiasm for what others are doing, the amount of time you spend helping others with their work, or certain other behaviors? To obtain useful information, you will need to be very specific about what you want to know. Lack of precision can cause others to be equally imprecise in the information they provide. Next, if you ask for feedback, you should be prepared to hear out the person who is trying to help. Do not interrupt or become argumentative. Sometimes it may take several days to see the wisdom of others' opinions. In addition, being receptive to both positive and negative comments will make others far more likely to offer candid and meaningful feedback in the future. Finally, try to solicit feedback from persons who are in the best position to judge your behavior objectively. Your attitudes in the classroom, for example, might be best evaluated by students. Do not underestimate their ability to be helpful. Researchers (Gage, 1963;

Tuckman and Oliver, 1968) have learned that teachers can initiate positive changes based on suggestions made by students.
Cultivate Interests Outside of School.   Many teachers report that
having interests outside of school facilitates developing and maintaining positive attitudes toward others. We agree completely. We
have found that we are most productive and agreeable when looking forward to a game of tennis or a night on the town. After
engaging in enjoyable events, we seem to appreciate our work and
other persons even more. If you look around at persons who respond most positively to others, you will probably find that these
persons engage in many different happiness-producing activities.

Do not misunderstand us. We are not saying that work is an
unenjoyable experience. Most of us derive much satisfaction from
our work. But most people need outlets from the occasional frustrations of their work. A teacher who relies solely on students and
colleagues for friendship may feel resentful if the students and
colleagues fail to be totally committed to the relationship. Attitudes
toward self and others can suffer. Our belief is that one should not
rely upon work for every satisfaction. If you have not already done
so, we suggest that you identify a number of activities that might
prove enjoyable to you (for example, reading, listening to music,
tennis, golf, swimming, hiking, jogging, gardening, crafts, and
similar activities). Establishing a time each day or week for participating in these leisure activities helps insure that one does not
become too busy for relaxation.

Attitudes Toward Self

Attitudes toward self and others are discussed separately in this
chapter. However, the two may be inseparable. Many prominent
psychologists (e.g., Combs, 1974; Fromm, 1947; and Rogers, 1961)
have suggested that our attitudes toward others are largely dependent upon the attitudes we hold about ourselves. You may have
noticed this relationship from your own daily experiences. For
example, have you ever performed poorly on a test or a teaching
assignment and then been harder to get along with? Everyone has
ups and downs and is easier to live with on some days than on
others. You may even have experienced a day now and then when
nothing seemed to go right. An occasional off day is not unusual.
Transient moods are seldom a real concern. It is habitual dissatisfaction that constitutes a threat to self and to others. You must

*"Mirror, mirror, on the wall, who's
the most sensitive, open, student-
centered, and innovative teacher of all?"*

avoid becoming so sensitized to the negative events in your life that
you completely overlook all the positive happenings. You could
easily join a league of individuals who comfort one another in
complaining about their problems, blaming others, and bemoaning
their fate. We do not want this to happen to you.

Assessing Your Attitudes

Just as you analyzed your attitudes toward others, you may wish
to make a self-examination of the attitudes you hold toward yourself before drawing any conclusions about needing to change. You
could begin by assessing your level of self-esteem. That is, how do
you feel about yourself as a person? Since self-thoughts and statements are components of self-esteem, examining these can yield
pertinent information. Are your self-thoughts usually positive or

negative? Do you make uplifting or derogatory remarks about yourself? Do you compare yourself favorably or unfavorably with most other people? Be honest. Even remarks that are seemingly made in jest can reveal how one actually regards oneself. In addition to raising questions about what you think and say about yourself, you might also ask how much confidence you have in your own abilities. The way one undertakes tasks can provide clues about self-confidence. Are you hesitant or enthusiastic about accepting responsibilities? Do you generally expect to be successful or unsuccessful in your work? Do you appear calm or anxious when presenting your views to others? Are you afraid to make decisions? Having skills in a teaching area is useless unless one has the confidence to put those skills to work.

Self-examination need not stop with an analysis of your self-esteem and self-confidence. You can make a personal inventory of many other attitudes. What about your attitudes toward learning, persistence, cleanliness, punctuality? How do your feelings on these matters affect the way you deal with others? Regardless of the attitude, our point is that you cannot do much about changing until you become aware of the attitudes you hold and how they are affecting your behavior.

Strategies for Change

Assessing self-attitudes by themselves may be insufficient for producing a change in attitudes or behavior. It may be necessary to implement a deliberate plan for self-change. The following are suggestions aimed primarily at altering levels of self-esteem and self-confidence. We are emphasizing these attitudes because they are important attributes for teachers. Similar strategies may also be used in altering other attitudes that are important in your personal affairs.

Think and Speak Positively about Yourself. Persons with high self-esteem or self-respect tend to think and speak favorably about themselves. Thus, altering self-thoughts and self-statements in a positive direction may change a teacher's feelings about self. This strategy has worked for others. Hannum, Thoresen, and Hubbard (1974), for example, worked with three elementary teachers who reported being too self-critical. The teachers kept a record of all their positive and negative self-thoughts during a specified hour each day. "I'm patient with children" and "I'm just too old for teaching" are examples of their positive and negative thoughts. Later on, the teachers were asked to increase the number of positive thoughts they made about themselves. The teachers were successful in doing so. Negative thoughts simultaneously declined. Two of the three teachers reported feeling markedly more positive about themselves, and referred to the experiment as one of the most significant events in their lives. Unfortunately, in this study, changes in self-esteem were not paralleled by immediate increases in positive actions towards the students. Such increases might require more time or additional strategies. A review of the literature on self-verbalizations (Michenbaum and Cameron, 1974) indicates that changes in self-thoughts are often accompanied by changes in overt behaviors.

Perhaps you might want to identify positive thoughts that could be used to change feelings. Thoughts about appearance, intelligence, and relationships with others would be appropriate. Listing these thoughts on index cards and referring to them at convenient periods during each day may be a helpful strategy. Referring to oneself more positively during conversations may also have a beneficial impact on self-esteem. Of course, you want to be discreet in what you say. There is a big difference between saying, "Yes, I was pleased with my performance" and "I did better than anyone else could possibly do." Being thought of as a braggart can create negative reactions and consequently lower feelings of self-esteem. But you need to get used to thinking and speaking positively about yourself. Just do not go overboard.

Accepting an honest compliment from others without downgrading self-performance can be a big step in increasing positive feelings toward oneself. People who feel negative about themselves may eventually find that others feel the same way toward them. Changes in self-confidence can be initiated by thinking and talking more positively about personal capabilities. Thinking that success is possible, that appropriate decisions can be made, that a classroom can be effectively managed fall into this category. The expectation of success is no doubt a prerequisite to actually doing a good job.

Finally, positive self-thoughts and statements may provide some immunization against the hurts that result from other people's comments and behaviors. Students can be especially cruel at times without even realizing it. All teachers occasionally have negative experiences. You must avoid letting those negative experiences adversely affect the way you think and act. We suggest that you focus primarily on the positive qualities that exist in oneself and in others. Remember, good things do not cease to exist when negative events occur.

Recognize Your Achievements.   We have found that many times people with low self-esteem and self-confidence completely forget about their past achievements. In new situations they fear they will fail or in some way prove inadequate. These people have undoubtedly had successful experiences in the past but the negative experiences have made the most lasting impressions. As a means of focusing on success experiences, it may be helpful to make a list of all the positive things that have happened and to review that list periodically. One teacher reported to us that she occasionally rereads all the positive notes she has received from her students over the years. She commented that when others can value her so much she just has to feel better about herself. Everyone has had success. Do not forget to recognize your own achievements.

Try New Activities.   Students and teachers can easily get into a rut. They may follow the same routine for studying or teaching for so long that all the excitement leaves their lives. To avoid that possibility, you may want to try something new from time to time. Try writing a theme a little differently from your normal pattern, develop a new set of lesson plans, or observe a new technique that someone else is using. Be willing to take a chance with new ideas. Admittedly, a certain amount of routine is good, but too much can diminish opportunities to grow and feel satisfied in making new achievements.

Avail Yourself of Educational and Therapeutic Opportunities.   Many teachers express a need for periodic rejuvenation. They report that the perplexities of the classroom seem to take their toll with time. Psychologists have even reported that teachers in inner-city schools sometimes exhibit the classic symptoms of combat fatigue (e.g., high blood pressure, disturbed sleep, depression, headaches). We find that reading professional texts, taking courses, and engaging in group experiences are helpful in reestablishing our positive attitudes. Other teachers tell us that they, too, seem more enthusiastic after exposing themselves to educational and therapeutic experiences. This strategy might work for you also.

Undergraduate and graduate courses oriented toward personal awareness are offered at virtually every college and university. Teachers can ask for, and usually get, in-service training courses that may be helpful in making attitudinal changes. Similarly, opportunities for participation in sensitivity groups are available in most communities. Such groups are interested in human relationships, and tend to emphasize honesty, openness of expression, trust in others, and the development of positive feelings toward self and others. We do not recommend these groups for everyone, but some people may derive benefits, especially increased self-awareness, from participation. One need not be inadequate in order to seek these opportunities for professional and personal growth. Quite the opposite. Truly professional individuals avail themselves of opportunities for self-improvement. Why not check out the possibilities in your school?

Concluding Remarks

Although this chapter has emphasized the importance of teacher attitudes, you still may be wondering how successful you can be in improving those attitudes. You also may be questioning Rogers' contention that certain teacher attitudes are sufficient to promote learning. We certainly feel that you can alter your present behaviors. What you are today is largely a function of your past experiences. What you are tomorrow just as surely will be a function of the things you experience today. We strongly oppose taking the "I'm just that way" philosophy. You can arrange today's experiences so that tomorrow you more closely approximate what you would like to be. We also doubt whether your attitudes alone, even though improved, will be sufficient for maximizing student learning. Other techniques for preventing and controlling classroom problems may also be necessary, perhaps because of our inabilities to achieve essential attitudes. Or, possibly our use of other techniques is necessitated because attitudes alone are not the only determinants of classroom behavior. In any event, we do not plan to ask you to rely solely on your personal charms. In succeeding chapters, a variety of strategies that can be used in conjunction with improved teacher attitudes will be discussed. By combining positive attitudes with other classroom management skills, learning may be made more pleasant for both students and teachers.

Suggested Projects

1. If you have not already done so, develop inventories for assessing your attitudes toward others and toward self, or combine the two into a single inventory.
2. Describe at least five behavioral changes that might be useful in improving your attitudes toward others.
3. Develop a plan that could be used in a classroom setting for altering your attitudes toward students. Your plan could include strategies for enhancing your listening skills or your knowledge of others' positive qualities, or some other behavior that you wish to change.
4. Describe at least three strategies that might prove helpful in altering self attitudes.
5. Develop a plan for enhancing your self-esteem and/or self-confidence.
6. Suggest that a period of time during a faculty meeting be designated for listening exercises. One helpful exercise involves pairing individuals who then carry on a discussion about a controversial topic. Before each individual is allowed to express his views, however, he must repeat to his partner's satisfaction what his partner has just said to him.

REFERENCES

Adams, R., and Biddle, B. *Realities of teaching: Explorations with video tape.* New York: Holt, Rinehart and Winston, 1970.

Bellack, A.; Kliebard, H.; Hyman, R.; and Smith, F. *The language of the classroom.* New York: Teachers College Press, 1966.

Combs, A. W. et al. *The professional education of teachers,* 2nd ed. Boston: Allyn and Bacon, Inc. 1974.

Fromm, E. *Man for himself.* New York: Holt, Rinehart and Winston, 1947.

Gage, N. L. "A method for improving teacher behavior." *Journal of Teacher Education* 14 (1963): 261–66.

Graubard, P. S.; Rosenburg, H.; and Miller, M. B. "Student applications of behavior modification to teachers and environments or ecological approaches to social deviancy." In E. A. Ramp and B. L. Hopkins (Eds.) *A new direction for education; Behavior analysis 1971.* Lawrence, Kansas: Support and Development Center for Follow Through, 1971.

Hannum, J. W.; Thoresen, C. E.; and Hubbard, D. R., Jr. "A behavioral study of self-esteem with elementary teachers." In M. J. Mahoney and C. E. Thoresen (Eds.) *Self-control: Power to the person.* Monterey, California: Brooks/Cole Publishing Company, 1974.

Klein, S. S. "Student influence on teacher behavior." *American Educational Research Journal* 8 (1971): 403–21.

Meichenbaum, D., and Cameron, R. "The clinical potential of modifying what clients say to themselves." In M. J. Mahoney and C. E. Thoresen (Eds.) *Self-control: Power to the person.* Monterey, California: Brooks/Cole Publishing Company, 1974.

Rogers, C. R. *Freedom to learn.* Columbus, Ohio: Charles E. Merrill Publishing Company, 1969.

_____ *On becoming a person.* Boston: Houghton Mifflin Company, 1961.

Sherman, T. M., and Cormier, W. H. "An investigation of the influence of student behavior on teacher behavior." *Journal of Applied Behavior Analysis* 7 (1974): 11–21.

Tuckman, B. W., and Oliver, W. F. "Effectiveness of feedback to teacher as a function of source." *Journal of Educational Psychology* 59 (1968): 297–301.

Williams, R. L., and Anandam, K. *Cooperative classroom management.* Columbus, Ohio: Charles E. Merrill Publishing Company, 1973.

CHAPTER THREE

SETTING THE STAGE
FOR DESIRABLE BEHAVIOR

The preceding chapter focused on the importance of positive teacher attitudes and attitudes toward self-change as prerequisites to effective classroom management. Positive teacher attitudes, however, do not insure that problem behaviors will never occur. Inappropriate behaviors may arise out of the situations to which students are exposed. Teachers who spend much of their time dealing with incident after incident of misbehavior would be well advised to consider whether conditions in the classroom are increasing the problems. If the factors that foster undesirable behaviors can be minimized, then classroom management problems can be reduced. In this chapter, a number of strategies aimed at preventing the occurrence of misbehavior will be presented. Strategies for increasing initial occurrence of desirable behaviors will also be included.

The procedures described in the following pages have been used successfully in actual classroom settings. However, any single technique in and of itself is unlikely to produce foolproof results. There are two major reasons why a particular technique may be less than 100 percent effective in all classrooms. First, a variety of complex variables is operating in any given classroom. What is appropriate in one class may be inappropriate in another simply because unnoticed, yet unique, differences exist between the two. Second, techniques are applied by people to people. All teachers do not apply strategies with the same enthusiasm nor do all students respond in the same fashion. Differences in individuality must be taken into account.

Having a variety of strategies for responding to classroom situations can be exceedingly useful, but rigid, mechanical application of the techniques should be avoided. Flexibility remains an important key in the use of any suggestion. If something works, fine. Make note of it. If a technique fails, be ready to evaluate why. Many techniques fail because they are misapplied. Above all, do not expect instantaneous results of perfection. Time is usually involved in producing worthwhile changes. Perfection is seldom achieved. Although teachers keep hoping, no one has yet developed a *perfect* solution for dealing with all behavior problems. Diligence in studying what others have done and in evaluating personal efforts will ultimately pay off.

Prompting Desired Behavior

One of the most effective means for preventing behavior problems in the classroom involves increasing desired student behaviors. Students obviously cannot behave appropriately and inappropriately at the same time. Therefore, you will want to rely heavily upon strategies that can initiate desired responses. A number of strategies do exist for prompting the kinds of behaviors most teachers would like to have students exhibit. These include: letting students know the rules, giving clear and simple instructions, making the setting conducive to learning, providing appropriate academic activities, and modeling desired behaviors. Strategies that can initiate desired responses are especially helpful in reducing the occurrence of classroom management problems.

Letting Students Know the Rules
Classroom Rules.   The establishment of class rules can serve as a means of prompting and guiding desired student behaviors. All teachers have certain general ideas about what students should or should not do. But these expectations are not always clearly understood by the students. We teachers sometimes assume that students come into classes knowing the rules of the game. This assumption is more likely to be made as students get older. However, teachers vary in what they expect from students. Different situations also call for different behaviors. These differences can create confusion for students. Too often students complain that they learn about the teacher's rules for conduct by unwittingly violating those rules. Students are not clairvoyant. They need to know what is expected so they can adjust their behaviors accordingly.

Although class rules can help prevent problems, the approach used to develop and make the rules known to students can easily

influence the results obtained. For example, a long list of regulations can give students the impression that the teacher is more
interested in increasing restrictions than in promoting learning.
A better approach is to keep the list to a minimum. Perhaps you
might initiate only those rules that are needed to keep your students from interfering with others' learning. We know one very
effective high school teacher who claims to have only two rules:
(1) You are to listen when I or any student speaks to the class, and
(2) You are to work so as not to disturb others. His approach is
simple but effective.

A class discussion might be a good starting point in developing
classroom rules. Involving students in decision making is especially important at the secondary school level. However, even very
young students can provide some ideas as to what makes a good
or bad class. A modified form of the strategies presented by Taba
(1966) for teaching cognitive skills could be used for conducting a
class discussion to generate workable ideas for classroom rules.
Initially, the procedure involves giving students a *focus* question
(e.g., "What do you consider to be appropriate or inappropriate
behavior in the classroom?"). After a student has responded, an
extended or a related question (e.g., "Why do you feel that throwing erasers in the classroom is not appropriate?") is asked. Students should be encouraged to explain and support their statements. For example, the teacher might say, "John, you state that
we do not need a rule about coming to class on time. Give me
some reasons why you think the class would operate better if we
did not have such a rule." Predictions (cause and effect) as to
classroom behavior if suggested ideas are or are not implemented
should also be elicited. Students may have divergent opinions on
some suggestions. All students should be encouraged to participate in the discussion and to defend their own beliefs about
proposed rules (e.g., "David, what do you think about the rule
proposed by Jerry?)." The discussion should be structured to
generate student-developed rules that are acceptable to both the
teacher and the students.

In working with students toward establishing class regulations,
you will also want to be certain that the students understand what
they are supposed to do—not just what they are prohibited from
doing. Stating rules in the negative can leave a student in doubt
about appropriate alternatives. Therefore, it is generally best to
state rules so that the students know exactly what is expected of

them. For example, "Please listen carefully while instructions are being given," "Raise your hand and wait until you are called on before speaking," "When you finish your math, you should get a book to read" are much more indicative of what students are to do than merely telling them "Don't talk while I am giving instructions," "Don't blurt answers," "Be quiet after you finish your math." Giving the rationale underlying rules may also be helpful. Remember, rules are intended to guide appropriate behavior. Involving the students, making certain that students understand the rules, and helping them see the rationale for rules can be important steps in achieving success.

Madsen and Madsen (1974, p. 181) provided suggestions that may serve as additional guides for establishing classroom rules. These points seem especially appropriate for elementary school classes.

1. Involve the class in making the rules.
2. Keep the rules short and to the point.
3. Phrase rules, where possible, in a positive way. ("Sit quietly while working," instead of "Don't talk to your neighbors.")
4. Remind the class of the rules at times *other* than when someone has misbehaved.
5. Make different sets of rules for varied activities.
6. Let children know when different rules apply (work-play).
7. Post rules in a conspicuous place and review regularly.
8. Keep a sheet on your desk and record the number of times you review rules with class.

Letting students know what is expected of them is critical to establishing effective classroom discipline, but one would be unjustified in assuming that rules *per se* will prevent all behavior problems. Teachers who feel that rules are ends in themselves usually become disillusioned when rules prove ineffective. Whether a student will be influenced by a rule depends largely upon what happens following compliance with or violation of rules. In at least one study, researchers (Madsen, Becker, and Thomas, 1968) found that rules alone had no appreciable effect on inappropriate behaviors. However, marked improvements occurred when rules were paired with teacher praise for appropriate behaviors and ignoring of minor inappropriate acts. The discussions in subsequent chapters should further clarify the importance of praising students for doing what is expected of them.

School rules and policies. In addition to classroom rules, it is important that students be cognizant of school regulations and policies that have a direct bearing on their conduct. Are certain school rooms off limits at certain times during the day? Is smoking permitted on school grounds? How many absences or times tardy are allowed before an attendance teacher is consulted? Questions of school policy are especially important for secondary school students. Discussing the regulations with students and posting a copy in the classroom to allow for continued reference may be helpful in reducing the number of rule infractions. Providing each student with a small handbook or a xeroxed copy of school policy is also recommended. Taking the time to discuss the policies during class periods will provide an opportunity to stress the positive aspects of the policies, thus increasing the probability that the desired behavior will occur. A discussion period will also allow students to vent any feelings they might have toward certain restrictions. In cases where rules are felt to be unfair or unnecessary, students can be helped to work within the school structure to effect a satisfactory change.

ALLOWING STUDENTS TO USE
THE LIBRARY BEFORE SCHOOL

One of the school policies at P.S. 34 involved hours when the library was open to students. The rule prohibited students from using the library before and after regular school hours. The library was open only when Mrs. Flynn, the librarian, could supervise. Students continually expressed dissatisfaction with this policy, stating that they were unable to complete assigned research during the school hours. In addition, many students rode school buses that dropped them at school thirty to forty-five minutes before the first period. This waiting time was felt to be wasted.

Mrs. Scott, in discussing school regulations with her students, found strong dissatisfaction with the library rule. She suggested that the students formulate a positive, workable alternative to be presented to the student council. The recommendation eventually made by Mrs. Scott's students suggested that students be recruited and trained as library staff members and that parent volunteers be solicited to supervise the library for one half hour before and after school. Students would be allowed to use the library during these times after obtaining a pass from the teacher who was on bus duty for the day. The procedure was eventually worked out with the librarian, principal, and student council members with the added stipulation that misbehavior in the library would result in suspension of before- and after-school library privileges for two weeks.

Student input about this school rule resulted in a decrease in grumbling about "not having a chance to use the library" and in an increase in the number of reports handed in on time.

Students often learn school rules by experience. That is, they may break a rule before they are aware of its existence. Questions of school policy should not be ignored by the classroom teacher. A frank discussion with students is recommended.

Giving Clear Instructions

Closely related to the suggestions about making rules explicit is the need to give clear instructions to students. Rules can provide a general guide as to what is expected in the classroom, but a rule cannot be initiated every time students are to perform a task. Providing clear and simple instructions can sometimes eliminate the need for elaborate behavior management programs. We have known teachers who set up elaborate systems for managing students when a simpler approach would have been to tell the students, "This is what I want you to do...." Simple approaches should be tested before initiating more complicated techniques.

Clear, simple instructions are fundamental to prompting desired behaviors. Lovitt and Smith (1972) indicate that teachers deliver several hundred instructions a day. They note that some students perform inadequately because the instructions have not been given precisely and consistently. For example, telling a student "Improve your work," "Give more thought to the issue," or "Think before you act" are too broad to prompt desired behaviors. These instructions may only result in students' becoming frustrated and perhaps disruptive. A more instructive comment would be, "John, your writing could be improved by giving more examples for each of the points you mentioned in your theme," "Jane, what do you think about including... position in your debate?" "Bill, why don't you check the correctness of your work by performing the reverse operation ... before you hand in your test?" Taking the time to be precise has the added advantage of letting students know that a teacher really cares about their work. Perhaps examining how the following instructions were made more specific will further assist you in evaluating the kind of instructions you give.

In addition to preciseness, you will want to provide consistency in giving routine instructions so that students can be sure about what they are to do. Changing the wording or emphasis of in-

UNCLEAR INSTRUCTIONS	CLEAR INSTRUCTIONS
1. Come in early in the morning and finish your chemistry test.	Come in at 7:45 a.m. and finish your chemistry test.
2. Show more team spirit.	Cooperate with team members by allowing other players to score rather than always attempting to run the ball. Show you are a team member by cheering other players on.
3. Make the school proud of you.	During the band competition sit quietly while other bands are playing: do not boo or yell; follow all instructions from your chaperons and play your best during the concert. Be a good winner by not boasting and ribbing other bands, or be a good loser by congratulating the winning band.
4. Show you have some responsibility.	Demonstrate responsibility by completing your homework assignments without being reminded.
5. Show you have some manners during lunch.	Use your napkin. Keep your elbows off the table. Chew your food before swallowing. Swallow your food before talking.
6. Don't take too long in the bathroom.	You have five minutes to go to the bathroom before you board the bus.
7. Don't be so immature.	Spitwads are not to be thrown during Algebra II class. Note passing is not allowed during class discussions.
8. Don't get too far from the building during recess.	Stay on the asphalt area during recess. Stay inside the fence during recess.

structions can create unneeded problems. One way to improve both the precision and consistency of your instructions is to ask students for feedback about how well points are being communicated. In working with slower students, it may be helpful to ask them to explain what they have been instructed to do. This technique often clears up sources of miscommunication. A teacher should also give instructions only when students are paying attention.

Making the Setting Conducive to Learning

Much appropriate and inappropriate student behavior is partly a function of environmental events that serve as cues for different kinds of behaviors. For example, you may have noticed that a certain student will work diligently when placed with one group of students but behave disruptively when placed anywhere near another group. You may have also noticed that when desks are lined up in straight rows, students often fail to interact freely during group discussions. Or, you may have learned that the time of day for presenting materials of differing difficulty levels has an influence on how well students pay attention. In these instances, group composition, seating arrangements, and time of the day have become important environmental cues affecting student behavior. Numerous other environmental stimuli such as lighting, temperature, and decor of the room can become the occasion for various student responses.

Part of a teacher's efforts in preventing classroom management problems should be aimed at arranging the setting so as to trigger desired student behaviors. This is not necessarily a difficult procedure. A first step is to identify the conditions that seem to increase appropriate behavior. Arrangements can then be made for them to be present on future occasions. Conditions that seem to serve as cues for inappropriate behaviors should also be identified and altered.

HAVING ASSIGNMENTS READY FOR STUDENTS

Mrs. McBride, a junior high math teacher, usually spent several hours each night grading papers and planning lessons for the next day. She never failed to have something planned for the students. But she seldom organized her materials so that she could get her classes started on time. Students would enter her classes and find that they had nothing to do for the first five or ten minutes. Mrs.

McBride would have to shuffle through a heap of papers, look around for the appropriate text, or search for her planning book in her desk. Meanwhile students talked with one another and occasionally got too noisy. Mrs. McBride would then have to admonish the class to get quiet. Disagreements sometimes then ensued between herself and the students.

Mrs. McBride decided to remedy the situation by preparing a mimeographed sheet that contained the lesson activities for each of her classes. This took her about five extra minutes each morning. She then handed an assignment sheet to each student as he entered her class. The strategy proved effective in prompting desired student behaviors and in reducing the major problem.

Managing the classroom.   Some of the most important cues that students receive about how they can or should behave come from the way the teacher manages the class. Kounin (1970), in his studies of classroom discipline, identified and categorized a number of these classroom management skills. For example, he found that what he called *withitness, overlapping, momentum* and *smoothness,* and *group alerting* were each related to freedom from misbehavior. Kounin used the term withitness to describe teachers who communicated through their behaviors that they knew what was going on in the classroom. Teachers with a high degree of withitness make few errors in correctly identifying who is misbehaving or in responding before misbehavior spreads or becomes more serious. Such teachers are also less inclined to make mistakes by responding to minimal disruptions while overlooking more serious infractions. Occasionally glancing around the room, arranging seats to provide a view of all students, and moving about the room should improve one's knowledge of what is going on in the classroom. Teachers who are in doubt about whether they need to be more "with it" might ask themselves: Have I frequently been accused by students of rebuking the wrong person? Have students got into serious problems over incidents that could have been prevented by my acting when the students were still kidding around? Do students make complaints such as . . . can get away with "murder" but you fuss at me for just whispering?

As Kounin used the term, overlapping indicates an ability to handle two situations simultaneously without becoming so immersed in one that the other is neglected. Teachers must be careful not to overlook students who need assistance, but must also be

"I see by your records that you were on that new degree program – having a major in classroom organization and rapport and a minor in education."

careful not to become sidetracked. You may find that you can give individual help to a student after the other students have been given an assignment. At other times, you have to assign a different task to the student until more time can be devoted to providing individual assistance. Neither an individual student nor a large group can be arbitrarily put off on too many occasions. To do so may communicate a lack of interest and unwillingness to assist the student. Care in planning and increased knowledge of subject matter should increase a teacher's ability to handle multiple tasks simultaneously. Teachers who are concerned about their own overlapping skills might ask themselves: How often have I turned my attention away from one student or group to another without at least giving the temporary instructions to the first group? How often do I say "not now" to a student who needs help?

As defined by Kounin, momentum involves keeping the learning activities free of slowdowns, whereas smoothness refers to the absence of teacher behaviors that interfere with the flow of learning activities. Kounin noted that overdwelling (nagging) about a behavior, materials, or a task and fragmenting an activity into parts (e.g., asking children to do separately what they could be asked to do as a group) can create unnecessary slowdowns. Examples of teacher jerkiness (anti-smoothness) provided by Kounin include: becoming easily distracted by irrelevant stimuli; bursting into an activity without considering the students' readiness for an interruption; abruptly dropping an activity, going off and then returning to the activity; and terminating an activity, starting something else, and then returning to the first activity.

AN EXAMPLE OF TEACHER ANTI-SMOOTHNESS

Sam had been absent from his tenth grade geometry class for three days due to illness. Two days after he returned, all students were assigned seatwork for practice in applying what they had learned during the class discussion. Mr. Miles asked to check Sam's makeup work to make sure that he had mastered the material he missed during his absence from class. Sam brought the work to Mr. Miles's desk and watched him begin to grade the papers. Mr. Miles noted that Sam had apparently misunderstood how to work a particular problem and began to explain how to approach it. In the middle of his explanation, two girls came to the desk and inquired about a project for selling shakers at a football game. Mr. Miles called the class to attention and made an announcement about the project. Several students asked questions and a general discussion resulted. Meanwhile, Sam went back to his seat. After the discussion was over, Mr. Miles called Sam back to his desk and asked "Okay, now where were we?"

You can probably think of many specific teacher behaviors that could facilitate momentum and smoothness in learning activities. What about having audio-visual equipment checked out and in place before using them in class? Few things can be more distracting to students than having a teacher work to repair a projector while they are waiting to see a film. Having lesson plans in a specific place, knowing where art supplies are located, developing strategies for moving students from class to class or to different locations in the classroom, and having sufficient copies of duplicated materials can also reduce lulls and unnecessary confusion during class and during transitions. Checking the actual lesson against the prepared plan for the lesson can provide teachers with a simple measure of how well they are able to maintain momentum in teaching activities. Finally, Kounin found that group alerting, that is, keeping nonreciting students involved and on their toes, is significantly related to freedom from deviancy. He observed that group alerting might be achieved by maintaining suspense about who is going to be called on, calling on different students frequently, creating interest in what is going to be asked (e.g., "This might fool you."), letting nonperformers know they may be called on in connection with what someone else has said, and introducing novel ideas into recitations. Kounin also noticed that holding students responsible for tasks going on during recitations is related to work involvement and freedom from deviancy. How predictable are you regarding who will be called on? Do you wait until a question is asked before identifying who is to respond? Once a student has been called on, can he expect to be overlooked on subsequent questions? Do you circulate and check the work of those who do not respond? How much attention have you given to keeping students on their toes and a part of the learning experience?

Skills related to withitness, overlapping, momentum and smoothness, and group alerting are obviously not the only classroom management skills that can prompt desired behaviors. Making certain that each child can see the chalkboard, spending some time improving the physical appearance of the room, controlling the number of interruptions from outside sources, and providing appropriate academic materials, to name just a few, can also prompt the kinds of behaviors desired by teachers. Because of the importance of academic materials, that topic will be discussed separately in more detail. The point is that the environmental conditions in the classroom can make a substantial difference in how students behave.

Providing Appropriate Materials
As axiomatic as it may seem, another principal means for prompting desired student behaviors is the provision of academic work at appropriate levels of difficulty. Teachers sometimes talk about poor attention span, restlessness, and lack of interest as though students were predisposed to those behaviors. It is more self-assuring to think that students have the problem than to be-

lieve that the class itself is boring or unexciting. The truth is that some students do misbehave because they have become bored with the lesson activities. Lessons that are too easy, repetitious, and routine can easily lead students to seek other things to do. Conversely, work can also be too difficult. Some students may give up and misbehave simply to avoid undertaking tasks that they know are far beyond their present skills. Students may feel that they can "save face" by being disruptive rather than undertaking and failing at impossible tasks. At least, a disruptive student can say, "I could have done it if I had really wanted to." Apparently, desired behaviors cannot be prompted by asking the same thing of all students.

BOB TRIED BUT JUST COULDN'T QUITE DO IT

Bob was repeating a required high school course in biology. He seemed interested in the work at first. He even told Mr. McGalliard, his biology teacher, that he really planned to try hard this year. Bob brought his book to class every day during the first grading period. He appeared to listen intently to the lectures and created no disturbances. But he performed miserably on the exams. Eventually, he began to show less interest. He started teasing the girls who sat close to him, and soon was a constant source of disruption. One day Mr. McGalliard asked him to read a short passage from the text. Bob slammed the book closed and stormed from the class.

Later, when Mr. McGalliard went through Bob's school record, he discovered that Bob was a very poor reader. Mr. McGalliard immediately changed the text that Bob was using. He also started giving oral exams to Bob and other students who were having similar problems. Bob's work slowly improved and by the end of the term he had earned a D for the course.

Not all stories have an ending even as happy as the one above. Providing stimulus materials at appropriate difficulty levels for every student is a major task. You may never completely achieve the degree of success that you seek. Continuous evaluation, planning, and flexibility are required. We know of no easy way the task can be achieved. But we do have a few suggestions that may prove helpful in guiding your efforts.

Evaluate present skill levels.   Before instructional plans are developed, the skill levels at which each student is working ought to be determined. If a class is large, an adequate educational diagnosis may require several days. However, the evaluation period will eliminate time lost from starting students on skill levels that are much above or below current levels of functioning. Subsequent classroom management problems may thus be prevented. You will find that many commercial tests, and those that you develop, can be administered to the entire class at the same time. Other tests, such as reading instruments, may need to be administered individually. Sometimes a handicapped student may require individual testing. With planning, however, even teachers of large classes should be able to include some individual testing in their evaluation period. Students who are not actively involved in the diagnostic process at any given time can be involved in other planned activities. For example, short encyclopedia reports, bulletin boards related to selected topics, art, reading, and independent study to be followed by short class discussions are activities that can be instructive and exciting enough to maintain the interest of most students. A great deal of useful information regarding work habits and ability to work cooperatively with others may also be gleaned from these less formal activities. And, while our suggestions may require a few hectic days for you, formal instruction in content areas is likely to be enhanced as a result of the preliminary diagnostic process.

Consider the use of programmed materials. After you have completed the preliminary diagnosis, you will undoubtedly have to do some planning to take care of individual differences among students. Seldom will every student in your class possess the same skills. One of the most useful strategies for dealing with individual differences involves using programmed materials. They present information in small steps, progress from easy to more difficult, demand active participation from the students by requiring an overt response (usually a written resonse to a question), and offer feedback on performances. Such materials permit students to work at their own pace and almost assure the students of success. Published programmed materials are currently available for practically every subject. It would be unrealistic, however, to assume that the majority of teachers have a variety of programmed materials available to them for use in the classroom. A growing number of teachers have therefore become involved in developing their own individualized programs. Teacher-made programs typically include (1) identification of the concepts, skills, or values that students are to learn, (2) objectives that state how the students must demonstrate mastery of the material, (3) provision of a variety of activities from which students can select to reach the objectives, (4) pretests that determine who really needs to study the materials, (5) directions regarding how to proceed, (6) posttests to determine how well the objectives have been attained, and (7) enrichment activities for students who desire further exploration on the unit of study.

You have probably surmised that you would not be able to sit down over a weekend and prepare programmed materials for your classes. Much more effort is required. You might find it beneficial to attend a summer workshop on developing individual programs. Such workshops usually allow time for participants to begin developing materials for use in their classes. Or, you could suggest an in-service training course for your school. Some teachers have found that the best way to proceed with the development of individualized materials is to join forces with their colleagues and prepare the materials together. Although the task will be time-consuming, you will be able to reach far more students once you have developed individual programs on a range of topics. You can also use the materials more than once.

Consider skills grouping.   Providing appropriate materials does not mean that you must work with only one student at a time. Another possibility for meeting individual differences is to arrange for skills grouping in your classes. The skills groups can vary depending upon student interests, needs, and readiness to undertake the tasks. Be assured that we are not advocating the establishment of permanent groups. That approach is unacceptable because no two students are going to have identical abilities for every task. As new activities are initiated, students with different skill levels should be grouped according to their differences. The composition of such groups should remain flexible so that students can move freely in and out of different groups as specific skills are mastered. For example, if the class is mathematics, a student might move to a group studying division of fractions only after achieving success with multiplication of fractions. As you can see, flexibility in grouping necessitates considerable planning for the teacher, but the strategy ensures that students are presented with appropriate assignments. The work is hard, but the alternative of failing to plan for individual differences is failure for some students.

Use variety in teaching.   While the provision of appropriate materials can have a major impact on student behaviors, doing the same thing day in and day out can present problems. The following case illustrates what can happen with too much repetition.

WHY CAN'T WE ...?

Mr. Copeland and Mrs. Shoemaker both taught French II classes. Mrs. Shoemaker had taught for several years and had her lessons for the year well outlined. Vocabulary lists, grammar worksheets, selections from the textbooks, and drill in pronunciation formed the mainstay of her teaching activities. One day she overheard several students in her class say that students in Mr. Copeland's class had more fun. She overlooked the comments, feeling that French was a serious subject.

Mary Jane eventually got up enough courage to ask in class why the students were never allowed to do anything different. Mrs. Shoemaker decided to look at her lesson plans objectively to see whether she could vary the way she taught the material. She met Mr. Copeland in the teachers' lounge later in the day and asked what techniques he was using that prompted so many positive student comments. She learned that Mr. Copeland devoted at least one day a week to teaching vocabulary and grammar in a unique way. For example, students made up crossword puzzles using French words and then exchanged puzzles with other students. Or they developed and acted out short scenes in French. Mrs. Shoemaker began to realize that she was relying too heavily on lessons she had used for years and that her lessons contained very little variety. She and Mr. Copeland decided to spend time together planning new activities for teaching French II.

No set of materials or teaching approach *per se* is sufficient to maintain the interests of students indefinitely. Having a variety of materials and methods is probably the best way to maintain maximum interest in school activities. As a matter of fact, Kounin (1970) found that variety and challenge in seatwork were significantly related to students' behavior in a learning setting. The use of movies, discussion groups, academic games, and group competition may serve as viable breaks from the routine, and prove to be useful learning activities in and of themselves.

Consider student interests.   The importance of student interests should be included in any discussion of providing appropriate materials. One's efforts may prove fruitless if students have no interest in what is offered to them. The common lament, "These students have no interest in learning," probably is not entirely true. The students may only be uninterested in studying what the teacher has in mind. A number of things can be done to combat this seeming lack of interest. First, and possibly the most important, students can be given some choice. There is some data (Davis, 1971; McEwen, 1972; Ryan, 1965) to show that students' choice of activities produces higher achievement levels than teacher choice of activities. Students at all age levels can be given some choice even if that choice is nothing more than selecting between two possibilities. Second, student interest in activities can often be heightened by the way the materials are introduced. Indicating how a topic is relevant to a student's occupational goals, presenting seldom recognized and stimulating thoughts, behaving enthusiastically, and associating the materials with other events known to be interesting to the students could have an impact on how interested the students become. Third, students' existing interests can be used to involve them in academics. Suppose a teacher knows that a student has an interest in automobiles. That student could be asked to read about racing, to study how the automobile has contributed to society, to report on the occupations related to the automobile, and to investigate how geometric designs are involved in automobile engineering. The student's interest could trigger appropriate academic endeavors in any number of disciplines. Students do not lack interest. However, their interests are often overlooked in prompting other behaviors.

Modeling Desired Behavior

Another procedure that can be exceedingly helpful in prompting desired student behavior is the planned use of role modeling. Individuals acquire much of their behavior by copying or imitating the behavior of others (models). This learning process is usually called role modeling or imitation. As a teacher, you have probably observed and imitated behaviors exhibited by some of your former teachers. You may have developed some good and bad teaching behaviors through imitation without even realizing that you were imitating others. Public school teachers may sometimes utilize the same strategies that were used by their college professors. The teaching styles that worked in college, however, may be totally inappropriate for a public school setting. Students, too, are constantly learning through imitation. They undoubtedly imitate more of their teacher's behavior than is expected. And they, too, can be acquiring some desirable and undesirable behaviors. With some forethought, modeling can be used advantageously.

There are several important ways in which modeling can be used to influence student behaviors and possibly prevent many classroom management problems. One tactic involves focusing attention on appropriate models in the class. For example, commenting that Joe and Bill are working together nicely allows students to see firsthand what is expected. Since this tactic is especially helpful in reducing disruptive behaviors, it will be discussed in more detail in Chapter Five. Our attention in this section will be devoted to the effects a teacher's behaviors can have on students.

Modeling critical behaviors. Suppose you scurry about the classroom, chatter constantly, and frequently find yourself yelling at the students. What influence will exhibiting such behaviors have on how your students react towards each other, how much self-control they demonstrate, or how they respond to learning situations? Suppose, on the other hand, that you begin walking about the room more slowly, stop chattering so much, speak softly, call students by name, and respond to them in more positive ways. How will these behaviors affect students? A teacher reported these conditions to Wesley Becker and his colleagues (Becker, Engelman, and Thomas, 1975), and noticed a dramatic improvement in student behaviors soon after she began setting a calmer example herself. You can probably think of numerous other teacher behaviors that serve as examples for the students to copy. Teachers who are enthusiastic, who demonstrate good work habits, and who are themselves polite and friendly quickly come to mind. Punitive teachers also have their effects. In fact, the extensive research efforts of Albert Bandura and his co-workers (1963, and 1969) clearly demonstrate that the behaviors of adult models have a pervasive influence on the way students behave.

MR. NORRIS CAN'T UNDERSTAND TODAY'S YOUTHS
Mr. Norris spends considerable time in the teachers' lounge discussing what has gone wrong with the youths of today. He generally concludes that students don't know what hard work means. According to him students have it soft. He believes that today's

students are much less productive than the students of his era.

Observation of Mr. Norris's own behaviors reveal that he seldom takes school work home with him. He frequently plans his own work or relaxes while students are given something to keep them busy. When asked to help with extracurricular activities, Mr. Norris usually has to decline because he "has to be out of town that night." Do you wonder why Mr. Norris's students seem so unproductive?

You may be thinking that no teacher can exemplify every worthy virtue. They cannot. Teachers are human, and, like everyone else, they have their faults. Nonetheless, teachers should not expect much success in getting students to exhibit behaviors that they themselves do not exhibit. A unique study by Bryan and Walbek (1970) illustrates the need for consistency between what individuals preach and what they practice. These experimenters exposed children to one of several types of models. Some children heard a model advocate giving a portion of his game winnings to charity. The model made no donation, however. Other children heard the model complain about giving, but the model did make a donation. The children's experimental opportunities to give a portion of their game winnings was influenced by what the models *did*, not what the models *said*. "Do what I say, not what I do" is simply an unworkable admonition. Teachers who are perplexed about why students behave as they do will surely want to examine their own behaviors for clues. A teacher is not expected to be perfect, but those behaviors desired from students should be modeled.

Crucial variables. A number of variables can influence how effective a teacher will be in getting students to imitate modeled behaviors. First, students are influenced by the perceived status or prestige of the model. Students are more apt to imitate someone who has status than someone who has not. Thorough preparation, demonstrated expertise on a particular topic, activities undertaken during and after school, friendliness, and a host of other behaviors could affect how much status or prestige students attribute to the teacher. Second, perceived similarity between the teacher and students can greatly enhance the modeling process. This does not mean one should dress like the students, wear their hair styles, or hang out with them. Students can see through superficial attempts at trying to be "just one of the gang." Admitting mistakes, requesting assistance from other, and laughing together with students at a funny story could reflect a similarity between a teacher and students. Students need to know that teachers are human and not paragons of virtue who share little in common with others. Third, personal attitudes toward students may influence whether one is imitated. Feshback (1967), for example, has pointed out that students are more prone to imitate teachers who respond positively than those who respond negatively to incorrect responses. If students have been accustomed to negative approaches, one probably should avoid coming on too fast with positive techniques. Gradual changes would be better. Finally, students are most likely to imitate behaviors that can be demonstrated in a clear and simple fashion. Trying to shoot over the heads of students or to impress them with new-found knowledge is not only poor teaching, but reduces the possibility of influencing students in other ways. Being a good example requires conscious effort on the part of every teacher. However, most teachers possess the necessary skills to model desired behaviors.

Evaluating Your Approach

We have now discussed a number of techniques for prompting desired student behavior. The following sample evaluation form summarizes our suggestions for using these techniques. The form is designed to provide data as to how the strategies are implemented and how well they work in the classroom. You may want to use our form for evaluating use of the strategies in your classroom. Or you may wish to develop your own evaluation form.

Focusing on the Students

Much of what has already been suggested is aimed at keeping the students at the center of the learning process. For example, providing a setting that is conducive to learning, using individualized programs, offering learning materials that are varied, interesting, and challenging, help keep the students foremost in the classroom. Nonetheless, the teacher's position of being the person in charge of the class can potentially pose a problem. Giving directions, having others listen attentively, and being asked for advice can sometimes result in classroom activities becoming focused around the teacher. As you will recall from the preceding

EVALUATION FORM FOR PROMPTING DESIRED BEHAVIORS

Strategy	Application	Yes	No	Results and Recommendations
	Did you remember to:			
A. Let the students know the rules	1. keep rules to a minimum?			
	2. involve students in making the rules?			
	3. make different rules for different occasions?			
	4. state rules positively?			
	5. review the rules periodically?			
	6. give students a copy of the rules?			
	7. post a copy of the rules?			
B. Give clear instructions	1. avoid vague terminology?			
	2. specify precise behaviors?			
	3. maintain consistency in giving routine instructions?			
C. Make the setting conducive to learning	1. look for conditions that seem to increase appropriate behaviors?			
	2. look for conditions that seem to serve as cues for inappropriate behaviors?			
	3. change the conditions that cue inappropriate behaviors?			
	4. maintain an alertness to everything going on in the room?			
	5. handle multiple tasks simultaneously without becoming sidetracked?			
	6. plan your school day to allow for smooth transitions from one activity to another?			
	7. involve all the students during class discussions?			

D. Provide appropriate materials

1. evaluate present skill levels of your students?
2. consider using programmed materials to individualize instructions?
3. consider developing your own programmed materials to individualize instruction?
4. consider flexible skills grouping?
5. reevaluate and reassign students to groups as skill levels change
6. use a variety of materials?
7. use a variety of teaching methods?
8. use teaching materials and activities that are related to student interests?

E. Model desired behaviors

1. demonstrate behaviors in a clear and simple fashion?
2. behave positively toward the students?
3. refrain from acting in an aggressive manner?
4. occasionally volunteer to assist with activities that students especially enjoy?
5. demonstrate special areas of expertise for the students?
6. demonstrate an interest and concern for the students?

chapter, teachers frequently dominate class conversations and activities. Of course, there is a time for teachers to direct class activities, present information, and actually be the focal point in the learning. Too much teacher involvement, though, can result in students' feeling left out of the learning process. Negative feelings toward the teacher and the school may also be generated.

MR. CLARK LEARNS TO TALK LESS

Mr. Clark was a U.S. History teacher who was extremely enthusiastic about his subject. He could talk for hours about the Founding Fathers, the development of the U.S., politics, and so on. In fact, he did. Whenever students would ask a question, Mr. Clark would become so enthused that he often went on far longer than he should. His students would practically fall asleep waiting for him to come to a conclusion. They asked fewer and fewer questions as the year progressed.

Mr. Clark loved history and he wanted his students to develop an appreciation of their country's history. He also recognized what was happening to himself and to his class. He decided to reduce his own verbalizing by asking more questions of the students. Instead of asking for one word responses, something he had done in the past, Mr. Clark began to ask more *why* questions. He asked fewer *when* and *who* questions. Whenever students questioned him, Mr. Clark tried to keep his answer to one minute or less. He also began asking others to comment on questions from the class. He even began turning questions back to the student. He reasoned that a student who asks a question probably has something else to say. Students began to take a greater interest in the subject. Mr. Clark still enjoys talking but he is beginning to enjoy listening as well.

No one knows why some teachers come to dominate most activities in the classroom. It happens, however. And the results are often a decrease in learning and an increase in classroom management problems. Who is the center of attention in your classroom? Ned Flanders (1970) proposes use of the Flanders' Interaction Analysis Categories to investigate verbal communication in the classroom. The system is felt to be especially useful in recording the presence or absence of verbal behavior patterns. Flanders' Interaction Analysis involves coding verbal behavior into three basic categories: teacher talk, pupil talk, and silence. Teacher talk and pupil talk may be subdivided into initiation (e.g., beginning a verbal interaction or introducing something new) and responses (e.g., verbally reacting to comments of others). *Teacher talk* includes accepting feelings or ideas of pupils, praising or encouraging, asking questions, lecturing, giving directions, criticizing or justifying authority. *Pupil talk* involves response to the teacher and self-initiated talk. If you plan to log your own behaviors (or have a friend do the recording for you) you might pay careful attention to how much you accept student feelings and ideas, praise or encourage, and ask questions as opposed to how much time you spend lecturing, giving directions, criticizing others, and justifying authority. The former behaviors are apt to facilitate involvement of the students while the latter could be restrictive of student participation. Use of the interaction coding schedule during inservice or preservice education can help teachers improve classroom instruction. At that time, teachers would be most likely to get helpful feedback from others. Of course, the system at any time can assist teachers in becoming more aware of how both teachers and students are involved in the learning process. Readers who are especially interested in evaluating their own interactions with students can refer to Flanders' *Analyzing Teaching Behavior* for more information regarding use of the Flanders Interaction Analysis System.

Summary

This chapter has stressed a number of procedures that can be beneficial in preventing the occurrence of classroom management problems. Specifically, the chapter included information on the need to (1) prompt desired behavior and (2) focus activities around the students. The discussion on prompting desired behavior emphasized procedures that could be used in initiating desired student behaviors. The procedures discussed included letting the students know the rules, giving clear instructions, making the setting conducive to learning, providing appropriate academic materials, and modeling desired behaviors. These procedures were presented as starting points, not as ends in themselves. The section on focusing on the students emphasized the necessity for placing the students—not the teacher—at the center of the learning process. The Flanders Interaction Analysis System was suggested as a possible means of improving classroom instructions.

As was mentioned earlier in this chapter, no single technique by itself is likely to produce any substantial changes in the classroom.

However, when procedures are combined into a total education program that reflects a general concern for the welfare of the students, dramatic changes should occur. A teacher may need to make only minimal changes to prevent some of the problems that tend to make teaching less desirable. The willingness to explore alternatives and to examine one's own approach to teaching is certainly a step in the direction of having a well managed class.

Suggested Projects

1. Arrange a class meeting to discuss with students what they believe to be appropriate and inappropriate behavior for that class. You might want to follow Taba's guidelines for conducting the discussion.
2. Reword the following instructions so that they are more precise: Don't talk unnecessarily, act like young ladies and gentlemen during the concert, don't be careless in your writing, dress appropriately for the dance, make sure you behave during assembly, try to do better in English IV.
3. Develop an individualized program covering a one-week unit of study. Be sure to include (1) an identification of the concepts, skills, or values that students are to learn, (2) objectives that state how the students must demonstrate mastery of the material, (3) provision of a variety of activities from which students can select to reach the objectives, (4) pretests that determine who really needs to study the material, (5) directions on how to proceed, (6) posttests to determine how well the objectives have been attained, and (7) enrichment activities for students who desire further explorations.
4. Make a list of all the class activities and materials that could be used for teaching a specific subject.
5. Secure the assistance of a colleague, school counselor, or school psychologist to record your interactions with students. You might want to use the Flanders Interaction Analysis Scale or another coding system.

REFERENCES

Bandura, A. *Principles of behavior modification.* New York: Holt, Rinehart and Winston, 1969.

Bandura, A., and Walters, R. H. *Social learning and personality development.* New York: Holt, Rinehart and Winston, 1963.

Becker, W. C.; Englemann, S.; and Thomas, D. R. *Teaching I: Classroom management.* Chicago: Science Research Associates, 1975.

Bryan, J. H., and Walbek, N.H. "Preaching and practicing generosity: Children's actions and reactions." *Child Development* 41 (1970): 329–53.

Davis, M. *Some effects of having one remedial student.* Paper presented at the 3rd Annual Kansas Conference on Behavior Analysis in Education, Lawrence, May, 1972.

Feshback, N. D. "Effects of teacher reinforcement style upon children's imitation and preferences." *Proceedings of the 75th Annual Convention of the American Psychological Association* 2 (1967): 281–82.

Flanders, N. A. *Analyzing teacher behavior.* Reading, Mass.: Addison-Wesley Publishing Co., 1970.

Kounin, J. S. *Discipline and group management in classrooms.* New York: Holt, Rinehart and Winston, 1970.

Long, J. D., and Williams, R. L. *Classroom management with adolescents.* New York: MSS Educational Publishing Company, Inc., 1973.

Lovitt, T. C., and Smith, J. O. "Effects of instructions on an individual's verbal behavior." *Exceptional Children* 38 (1972): 685–93.

Madsen, C. H., Jr.; Becker, W. C.; and Thomas, D. R. "Rules, praise, and ignoring: Elements of elementary classroom control." *Journal of Applied Behavior Analysis* 1 (1968): 139–50.

Madsen, C. H., Jr., and Madsen, C. K. *Teaching/Discipline: A positive approach for educational development,* 2nd ed. Boston: Allyn and Bacon, Inc., 1974.

Mager, R. F. *Preparing instructional objectives.* Palo Alto, California: Fearon Publishers, 1962.

McEwen, J. H. "An examination of the effects of manipulating setting events on the behavior and academic achievement of secondary school students." Ed. D. diss., The University of Tennessee, 1972.

Ryan, T. A. "Testing instructional approaches for increased learning." *Phi Delta Kappan* 46 (1965): 534–36.

Taba, Hilda. *Teaching strategies and cognitive functioning in elementary school children.* (Cooperative Research Project No. 2404, United States Department of Health, Education, and Welfare). California: San Francisco State College, 1966.

Williams, R. L. and Anandam, K. *Cooperative classroom management.* Columbus, Ohio: Charles E. Merrill Publishing Co., 1973.

CHAPTER FOUR

ACCENTING THE POSITIVE

To this point, our discussion has focused on procedures for initiating appropriate student behavior. The provision of rules, giving clear and simple instructions, making the setting conducive to learning, providing appropriate academic materials, and modeling were suggested as ways for prompting desired behaviors. As mentioned earlier, however, whether students will be guided by a rule depends largely upon what happens *after* they have displayed desired responses. The long-range effects of other prompts is also a function of what happens following the students' behavior. Students will not indefinitely continue following instructions, behaving appropriately in the classroom, or imitating a teacher's behavior unless their actions produce meaningful consequences. Psychologists have long cautioned that only those behaviors that produce pleasant consequences (positive reinforcers) tend to be repeated, whereas behaviors that have no noticeable effect on the environment are discontinued. In other words, persons continue performing both appropriate and inappropriate behaviors because of the consequences produced by those behaviors.

Making Desired Behavior Pay

The appropriate behaviors that a teacher would like to increase in the classroom are sometimes unintentionally discouraged. At the same time, inappropriate behaviors may begin to occur with distressing frequency. What happens to produce such clearly undesirable changes in students' behavior? An analysis of the events occurring in the classroom may reveal that the contingencies have been reversed. That is, the appropriate behaviors fail to receive a payoff, while the inappropriate behaviors are rewarded.

ASKING PERMISSION TO SPEAK

Mrs. Carter began preparation for a unit examination in her fifth grade American History class with a brief review. Most of the students had spent the previous week reading and working on projects related to their study and were well prepared for the test. The first question resulted in many students' raising their hands for permission to speak. However, before she could recognize one of these students, Max blurted out the answer. After commenting on the correctness of Max's answer, Mrs. Carter moved to the next question. Again several hands waved frantically in the air, but Jim quickly called out the answer. Mrs. Carter commended Jim for his excellent answer and praised the class as a whole for being so well prepared. She then continued the review by asking a third question. This time few hands went up. Instead, several students began to answer the question immediately. At this point, Mrs. Carter attempted to restore order by admonishing the students to remember the class rule: Raise your hand and be recognized before speaking out in class.

Unfortunately, the classroom example described above is not atypical. All of us at one time or another have probably observed a similar situation. What went wrong in this classroom? Something obviously happened to change the behavior of the students so that a classroom rule was disobeyed. The fifth graders would probably answer very simply, "If I raise my hand, I won't get to answer." In more technical terms, the teacher failed to reinforce desired behavior.

Appropriate behaviors occur frequently in every classroom. Students *do* remember to raise their hands before speaking. They *do* remember to bring their books to class. They *do* remember to complete their homework. But teachers sometimes forget how important it is to reinforce the behaviors they expect from students. Good behavior is often taken for granted. You may have given up on an idea, become totally discouraged, or struck out at someone because nobody seemed to notice how hard you were working. "What's the use?" or "Nobody cares" are familiar refrains. Students react the same way. The appropriate behaviors that teachers initiate in students must pay off or the behaviors will diminish. A key, then, to preventing many classroom management problems is to make appropriate behavior pay.

Selecting An Effective Reinforcer

The term reinforcer has been used several times in the preceding discussion. Psychologists use the term to refer to any stimulus or event that strengthens behavior. In this chapter, we are concerned with positive reinforcers, which are those events or items that strengthen (maintain or increase) the behaviors that they follow. Examples, for most people, include money, candy, good grades, and praise. The terms reward, payoff, and positive consequences are sometimes used in the place of the more technical term, positive reinforcer. In this chapter, these four terms may be used interchangeably.

At this point, you may be thinking that teachers often use positive reinforcers but still are unable to strengthen the desired behaviors of some students. You have undoubtedly heard teachers say, "I have tried everything with that student and nothing seems to work." Or, you may have heard teachers exclaim, "There is really nothing to positive reinforcement. It simply doesn't work." In many instances, the items or events used as payoffs may be reinforcing *only* to the *teacher*. The student may be turned off completely by what the teacher perceives as a reward. The fact that some events may be nonreinforcing to students can account for many of the "failures" in getting students to continue behaving in desired ways.

The most accurate way to determine whether an item will serve as a reinforcer is to present it following a behavior and observe its effect on the behavior. Remember, the presentation of a positive reinforcer will increase the frequency of the behavior that it follows. Presenting a potential reinforcer and observing its effects on behavior may not be the most efficient method of identifying reinforcers for classroom use, however. Time and effort may be saved in trying to improve classroom management if *potential* reinforcers are identified prior to implementing any new programs. One useful method for determining items that may serve as positive reinforcers in the classroom involves observation of the students. What activities do they engage in when they have free time? What books do they read? What games do they play? It is apparent that all students

TABLE 4–1

POTENTIAL REINFORCERS FOR CLASSROOM USE

Social Reinforcers	Activity Reinforcers	Tangible Reinforcers[1]	Token Reinforcers	Feedback Reinforcers
Teacher praise "Correct." "Very good." "I'm pleased for you." "Excellent idea." "Good job." "You're doing well."	Spelling contests Choosing a seat in the cafeteria Choosing a seat in the classroom Being a line leader Going to library Working on special projects Talking to others	Consumables M&Ms Cereal pieces Raisins Cokes Crackerjacks	Points Checkmarks Grades Poker chips Money[2]	Knowledge of results
Nonverbal approval Smile Hug Wink Pat on shoulder Nod	Arranging a bulletin board Answering doors and taking messages Being a group leader Class parties Athletic contests	Inexpensive toys Marbles Balloons Award buttons Baseball cards Puzzles Comics Magazines		
Being asked for one's opinion Recognition	Movies Field trips Being teacher's helper Free time for reading, games or other events Access to play area or special area in classroom			

[1]Tangible reinforcers are often used with special education students. These reinforcers may also be necessary in regular classrooms when students are not amenable to change through other approaches.

[2]May be provided by parents and used as a reinforcer in implementing change programs in the school.

do not choose to engage in the same activity. One student may eat a snack; another may read a book. *Events that are reinforcing to one student may not be reinforcing to another.* Given a choice, the student will engage in the activity that is reinforcing to him. Observation of students during free time periods should thus provide useful clues regarding potential reinforcers.

A second method for determining items that may serve as positive payoffs involves asking the students. The most direct method often turns out to be the easiest and most effective one. A class discussion can identify reinforcers that the teacher has failed to consider. Textbooks and articles dealing with classroom management may also yield ideas for possible rewards. Talks with other teachers can add additional possibilities. The potential reinforcers listed in Table 4–1 offers some ideas for the classroom teacher. You might try adding to our list.

Using Teacher Attention as a Payoff

Perhaps the most natural and readily available payoff for appropriate student behavior is teacher attention. A word of praise, a pat on the back, a smile, a friendly glance, or a wink can drastically improve relationships within a classroom and go a long way in minimizing classroom management problems. In fact, teacher approval has been widely used in reducing a variety of problems with elementary (O'Leary and O'Leary, 1972) and junior high and senior high school students (Long and Williams, 1973). Teacher approval has the apparent advantage of taking little time and effort. Certainly no more time or effort is involved in catching students being "good" than in catching them being "bad." But the systematic use of teacher attention is not quite as simple as it may appear. First, all students do not respond in the same way to teacher approval. Second, some teachers are unaccustomed to the systematic use of attention, especially in using their approval in meaningful ways.

Student reactions.   Teachers are occasionally surprised when their approval proves ineffective with certain students. Most students have learned to value praise and other forms of social approval because their parents coupled attention, praise, and smiles with food, warmth, comfort, and other important reinforcers. Some youngsters have had the misfortune of never having affection paired with things typically associated with a wholesome home environment. Such students may fail initially to respond in expected ways. The situation can be remedied, however, by repeatedly pairing approval with other known reinforcers. For example, a teacher might comment, "Bill, because you have been working so hard on your math assignment, you can line up first for lunch." Eventually, by preceding known reinforcers (e.g., special privileges) with teacher approval, approval should become a potent influence on student behavior.

Students may also respond atypically if the teacher's approval generates ridicule from peers. Public accolades occasionally result in students' being called teacher's pet. Praise under such circumstances only creates problems for the teacher and the students. The use of nonconspicious approval may constitute a better strategy. Comments on homework assignments, gestures, winks, and private comments may be just what is needed to help the student continue behaving appropriately. Most students relish approval when it is judiciously administered, but careful consideration should be given to how students react to your choice of verbal comments and nonverbal approval. Hugs and physical closeness, for example, may prove beneficial with elementary students, yet be disastrous with junior high students. Obviously, discretion should be used in selecting and administering approval.

Offering meaningful approval. Indiscriminate use of approval can conceivably produce an increase in unwanted behaviors. Students can also be turned off by the way approval is offered, especially if they interpret the praise as phony or insincere. A teacher can be totally honest in wanting only to recognize the accomplishments of students and yet be perceived as manipulative or artificial. For these reasons, we are offering the following suggestions (Williams and Anandam, 1973) for giving praise in an authentic and meaningful way.

  1. Praise significant behaviors. Students know when they have worked hard on a task and they know when they have expended little effort. Few students will welcome being praised on trivial matters. Of course, what is significant or trivial may vary from student to student. By observing students' work and by listening to them, a teacher should soon be able to offer some meaningful praise to *every* student.
  2. Be precise. Generally, the more specific the praise, the more reinforcing it will be. A student can be told that something is "great" or "very good" without much effort. Indicat-

ing what is particularly liked requires greater thought and attention. Perhaps that is why specific praise is more valued and less apt to be deemed insincere. Pinpoint the exact behavior that is being approved. "I liked your painting because . . ." "You got nine of ten problems correct; that's good work." "Your question about . . . raises some interesting issues."

3. Consider how you praise. A teacher can be so lavish in administering approval that what is said is minimized. Coming on too strong represents a common mistake in using praise. One need not be grandiloquent. A wiser strategy is simply to make the approval commensurate with the student's actual performance. A student can be told that he is working hard or that he did his assignment correctly without going to extremes in praising and without comparing his work with others'. Some of the most effective teachers are those who remain calm in recognizing the accomplishments of their students.

4. Avoid redundancy. Students can get tired of hearing a single word or phrase. They may also doubt the sincerity of a teacher who repeatedly uses only one form of approval. Try identifying and using many different words, phrases, gestures, facial expressions, and forms of contact for conveying approval. With practice, a teacher can become proficient in expressing approval in new ways.

5. Develop consistency between verbal and nonverbal behavior. The impact of verbal comments can be readily diminished by nonverbal actions. For example, telling a student "that's good work," while attending to something else, will not be nearly as effective as examining the work, looking at the student, and smiling while the approval is being given. Eye contact, closeness, attention, tone of voice, facial expression, and body movements tell students as much as words. Words are useless when nonverbal behaviors contradict what is being said.

6. Be consistent. Students need to know what they can expect. When students realize that they can depend upon a teacher to recognize and appreciate their efforts, the teacher is on the way to becoming an important influence in their lives.

7. Try a gradual approach. Abruptly increasing the amount of approval administered can make a teacher appear awkward or insincere. Students may interpret the change as an

indication that they can behave any way they choose. Give them a chance to adjust to the new approach. Approval can be increased as they increase their achievements. Other rewards can also be used in order to avoid overdoing verbal approval. Expressing approval is a basic means of reinforcing appropriate student behaviors. However, not all teacher approval is equally received by students. What is approved, how precise the approval is, the style, the choice of words, the consistency between verbal and nonverbal behaviors, the consistency in giving approval, and the frequency of approval can all add to or detract from the influence of the teacher. Effort in recognizing and controlling these factors should greatly enhance the overall effectiveness of approval both in strengthening desirable behaviors and in preventing classroom management problems. The benefits are numerous. The task is a relatively easy one for most teachers.

Using Other Reinforcers

Teacher approval, of course, is only one of many potential reinforcers available in the classroom. Any of the types of potential reinforcers identified earlier could strengthen desired student behavior. Asking students for their opinions, holding up an idea for further discussion, and giving students feedback about a performance can serve as potent reinforcers. Even tokens (e.g., points, poker chips) with the use of back-up reinforcers (e.g., free time privileges, consumables) may be used if less complicated and more natural classroom approaches prove ineffective. Items that serve as reinforcers may vary, depending upon the students and the situation. As mentioned earlier, the only way a teacher can be certain as to whether something is reinforcing is to assess its effects on the students. Different ideas can be tested to determine what works best in a particular classroom. It may be found that a combination of teacher approval, feedback, tangibles, and activity reinforcers is more helpful than the use of any single technique. Seldom will any one technique have the same impact on everyone. Through careful selection of reinforcers, teachers can help each student develop desired academic and social skills.

The Effective Use Of Positive Reinforcement

While care in selecting a reinforcer can be a critical element in strengthening the appropriate behaviors that students exhibit, careful attention must also be given to the way in which reinforcers are used. Indiscriminate use of positive reinforcement will seldom produce intended results. Fortunately, a number of well-known educators and psychologists (e.g., Kazdin, 1975; Krumboltz and Krumboltz, 1972; Piper, 1974; Wilson and Williams, 1973) have provided practical suggestions regarding the use of positive reinforcers. So let us turn now to the most frequently suggested strategies for using positive reinforcement to best advantage.

Specifying Target Behaviors
In arranging for the proper application of positive reinforcement, it is important that the behavior to be increased be clearly specified. Failure to pinpoint the desired behavior can result in a misunderstanding between teachers and students and may contribute to classroom management problems.

CLEANING UP AFTER SHOP CLASS
Mr. Smith was continually dissatisfied with the condition of the shop room following woodworking classes. Generally, the students were a cooperative group, but they invariably failed to clean up to Mr. Smith's satisfaction. Although they worked busily at the end of the class period, instructions to "leave the shop neat" did not appear to be carried out. A class discussion finally revealed the nature of the problem. The instructions to "leave the shop neat" had failed to communicate sufficient information regarding Mr. Smith's expectations. As long as the work tables were clear, the students considered that the shop was neat. Neatness as defined by Mr. Smith, meant that each tool must be put in its proper place. When the source of the misunderstanding was determined, he began to specify precisely what students were to do in order to "leave the shop neat." Thereafter, he was more pleased with the condition of the shop following class sessions.

Very little information is conveyed to students if the behaviors desired by teachers are defined in general terms. Precisely specifying desired behaviors has the advantage of bringing into focus for *both* students and teacher exactly what is expected or required. Miscommunication is less likely to occur if the desired behaviors are defined in terms that allow them to be counted. Telling John that he should do better work in spelling provides little direction regarding desired behavior change. Telling him that after studying Lesson Five he should be able to spell fifteen out of twenty words correctly on the weekly unit exam conveys exact information regarding the desired behavior. Whether the goal is to increase academic performance or to decrease inappropriate social behaviors, the overt behaviors that are desired should be specified.

Delivering Contingent Reinforcement
Once the target behavior has been clearly defined, reinforcers should be delivered only *after* the behavior has been exhibited. In other words, the reinforcer should be made contingent upon the desired behavior. Delivery of the reinforcer before, and not after, the performance of the desired behavior may have an unintended result. Consider the classroom example below:

ARITHMETIC BEFORE PLAY
Mr. Wilson, a sixth grade teacher, assigned fifteen arithmetic problems to be completed by the end of the class period. His students were told that the assignment must be finished before they would be allowed to go outside and participate in a volleyball game scheduled as a special treat. Nevertheless, a few students dawdled and wasted time on activities unrelated to arithmetic.

By the end of the period, twenty of the students had finished the assignment and went out to play. The ten students who had not completed their work asked permission to play also, insisting that the game was "special." At this point, Mr. Wilson relented. The dawdling students were allowed to go play volleyball but were admonished to complete their work as soon as the game was over. At the end of the school day, a check of each student's work revealed that only four of the ten students had completed the arithmetic assignment. The intentions of all the students were good. So were Mr. Wilson's. What went wrong?

The promises "I'll finish this after I . . ." and "I'll do it later" are often heard by classroom teachers. Teachers who acquiesce to these requests may be repaid by the students' failing to complete their work on schedule. Most teachers prefer not to appear cold and hardhearted. So they often reason, "What will it hurt if a student fails to complete the work just this once?" But a teacher's well-intended failure to make the reward contingent upon the appropriate behavior could easily result in students' being "taught" undesirable behaviors. In the classroom example described above, the reinforcer (i.e., the opportunity to participate in the volleyball game) was delivered even though assignments were not completed. The behavior that was actually rewarded for ten students was dawdling behavior. Sometimes being a "good" teacher requires saying no. One may not be very popular at that moment but helping students learn to manage their behaviors better will pay off later for everyone concerned.

Providing An Immediate Payoff

Many students, especially younger or slower ones, may lack the ability to delay gratification for very long. Thus, the promise of reinforcement in the future is insufficient to generate behavior change. The payoff for performing a desired behavior must be immediate. Failure to consider the effects of a delay in reinforcement may sabotage an otherwise well-planned program to improve classroom management.

MASTERING THE MULTIPLICATION TABLES

Mrs. Amherst, a fifth grade arithmetic teacher, decided to design and implement a behavior management strategy in order to fulfill requirements for an educational psychology course that she was taking in evening school. She elected to use bubble gum to increase the speed with which her fifth graders mastered the multiplication tables. According to her plan, each time a student learned and repeated without error a new set of the tables, he earned two pieces of bubble gum. The gum was scheduled to be distributed on Friday afternoon just before the final bell. Mrs. Amherst was careful to record the amount of bubble gum that was earned by each student. To her surprise, only a few students mastered more sets of the multiplication tables than they had during the previous week.

The importance of immediacy of reinforcement was overlooked in setting up the behavior change program described above. The reinforcer (i.e., the bubble gum) was not delivered soon after the desired response, but only on Friday. The increase in the number of multiplication tables repeated correctly on Friday attested to the efficacy of the gum as a reinforcer for many of the students. But reinforcement was delayed too long to be effective on the other days. As a result of the delay, satisfactory behavior change never occured.

You have probably surmised that the types of events being used as reinforcers may preclude immediate delivery in the classroom.

A basketball game with a competing seventh grade class may serve as an effective reinforcer for completing science projects, but the game obviously cannot be delivered each time a student turns in a project. When a reinforcer cannot be delivered immediately following the desired response due to unavailability of the reinforcer or disruption of classroom activities, other reinforcers such as points, stars, or check marks can be used to "bridge the gap" (Neisworth, Deno, and Jenkins, 1969). Tokens such as these may be delivered immediately and used to "buy" the other rewards. Willing teachers, then can usually find ways to make desired student behavior pay off without the loss of effectiveness and without disrupting classroom activities.

Reinforcing Often At The Beginning

When teaching new behaviors, it is desirable to reinforce them as frequently as possible in order to strengthen them and make them more likely to occur again. Generally, a procedure known as a continuous schedule of reinforcement is recommended for new behaviors and for those that presently seldom occur. Continuous reinforcement involves delivering a reward after each desired response. Teachers apparently cannot deliver continuous reinforcement for indefinite periods. They do not have the time. But they can deliver frequent reinforcement at first and then begin reinforcing on an intermittent schedule after the behavior becomes well established. Use of an intermittent schedule involves reinforcing only a percentage of the responses that occur, rather than all of them. Such reinforcement has the advantage of maintaining behavior for long periods of time, and minimizes the likelihood that individuals will tire of the reinforcer. By using continuous reinforcement to establish the desired behavior and intermittent reinforcement to maintain it, the advantages of the two procedures can be combined (Kazdin, 1975).

Rewarding Behavior Consistently

Students may become confused and disillusioned when a teacher is indiscriminate in the types of behaviors that are reinforced. Responding to appropriate behavior one day and providing the same consequence for inappropriate behavior on another day will seldom result in effective classroom management. Consistency in implementing a behavior change plan must be maintained.

REPORTING CURRENT EVENTS

Mr. Nate, a twelfth grade economics teacher, felt that it was very important for students to be aware of current information regarding the nation's economy and financial status. However, his requests that students read the daily newspapers and report the information in class were usually forgotten or disregarded. He therefore decided to reinforce the desired behavior by setting up a point system. Under his system, students could use points earned by bringing current events to class to buy free time for personal persuits. Students reacted enthusiastically to the plan and began to bring interesting articles to class.

Mr. Nate was very pleased with his students' responses to the point system. As a busy teacher, however, he often did not take the time to record the points when they were earned. Unfortunately, this failure led to frequent conflicts with students regarding the number of points they had actually earned. In addition, he sometimes awarded free time to all the students whether or not reports had been turned in. As a result, the number of current articles reported in class began to diminish.

If a teacher is unable to follow through in enforcing classroom rules and providing rewards as promised, students' behavior will reflect this lack of consistency by failing to change in the desired direction. Unfortunately, following through is the most difficult task in carrying out strategies to improve classroom management. One strategy for helping to increase consistency involves listing precise behaviors that are to be rewarded. Setting a specific time each day for record-keeping will increase the probability of following through with this aspect of a behavior change strategy. Being consistent is difficult. Nonetheless, the ability to maintain consistency remains a cardinal characteristic of an effective classroom manager.

More Difficult Situations

What has been said thus far is most applicable to students who readily display the behaviors desired by teachers. The teacher sets the stage, (i.e., establishes class rules) for desirable behavior, the student engages in correct behavior, and the teacher immediately provides a reward to strengthen the student's appropriate response. A few students may seldom emit the exact behaviors teachers want. And prompts *alone* may be insufficient for getting these students to exhibit the desired behaviors. Thus, the teacher may encounter difficulty in planning reinforcement for students who possess few of the social and academic skills that can earn rewards. However, a technique for enhancing the behavior of these students has been developed. Essentially, the procedure involves looking for and reinforcing crude approximations of desired behavior. Gradually, more complex behaviors are required and rewarded until the terminal goal is reached.

Rewarding successive approximations of a terminal goal rather than requiring its entire mastery before the reinforcer is delivered allows for individual differences among students. The procedure involving rewarding small increments of behavior change has been called "shaping." New behaviors can be created even though the one that the student can originally perform is only marginally related to the terminal goal. The first response to be reinforced may resemble the final goal or it may include only a small component of the terminal response. By reinforcing small steps toward the terminal response, that is, by requiring responses that are increasingly similar to the final goal before giving a reinforcer, the desired behavior is gradually achieved. Responses that do not approximate the terminal goal are not reinforced and thus are extinguished.

Strengthening Academic Responses

The shaping procedure is often used in teaching academic behaviors. Consider the method for teaching a child to print his name. For kindergarteners and very slow students whose skills are limited to drawing a circle, a square and a roughly drawn man, printing may be a formidable task. The task can appear more manageable if it is broken down into small steps that allow for frequent feedback and reinforcement. At the beginning, a child's name is printed on ruled paper and the child is given the opportunity to trace over it many times. When the child is able to trace accurately the letters of his name, he must more closely approximate the desired behavior by tracing letters that have been only faintly printed on the paper. Again, mastery of this step must be achieved before progressing to the next step, i.e., tracing the name over dotted lines. Cues are eliminated until the final goal of printing the name without prompts is achieved. The terminal goal is attained by beginning with a crude approximation of the desired reponse and gradually requiring more complex components of the terminal behavior. Prompting the response increases the probability that it will occur; "fading" the cues by gradual elimination increases the likelihood of a more independent response. In applied situations, fading and shaping precedures are often used simultaneously (Piper, 1974).

Strengthening Social Behaviors

The use of the shaping procedure is not limited to developing academic responses. Social behaviors, such as talking to others or volunteering in class, are also amenable to change using this process. An often overlooked classroom problem is the shy, withdrawn student who fails to participate in group discussions and who is seldom selected by peers to be included in group activities. With the more outgoing students clamoring for attention, that student may receive little or no reinforcement. Because the shy student usually does not volunteer to participate in class activities or group games, it may be necessary to use a shaping procedure in order to develop self-initiated participation.

In shaping behavior toward a terminal goal of volunteering to talk during class discussions, the first behavior to be reinforced should be one that has an element of the desired response. For example, looking at the teacher when a question is asked during a class discussion may initially be rewarded. It is important that the reinforcers be carefully chosen. Asking the student to answer the question may result in further withdrawal. Instead, a comment, such as "I'm pleased to see that you are interested in the discussion," may be more effective. Continuing to reinforce only attending behavior will not result in the establishment of the final goal, however. The next step will require rewarding a behavior that more closely approximates self-initiated participation. Raising a hand to answer when a question is asked represents a second step toward volunteering, and should be reinforced. After the student begins answering direct questions, reinforcers can be delivered for comments that are not direct answers to questions, e.g., "I'm pleased that you are sharing your thoughts on this matter." The shaping procedure should be continued until the student reaches the desired degree of participation in the classroom.

Reinforcement, of course, is a reciprocal process. As shy students become more outgoing, they receive more reinforcers and, as a result, increase their participation. They also deliver more reinforcers, thus increasing the probability that others will be interested in interacting with them. The teacher can further

*"Class, you will never know how pleased I am
to announce that each of you has been promoted."*

prompt social interaction by arranging classroom activities that
will require cooperative effort. Choosing an activity that a shy
student can perform well, and naming that student as group
leader, may also facilitate the process. If, for example, a shy student is proficient in art, his group might be assigned responsibility for advertising a class play. Most students like to have a "win-
ner on their team." In dealing with shy students, the points to
remember are simple: prompt the behavior, and reinforce small
steps toward the terminal goal.

In contrast to shy, withdrawn students, hyperactive students
are seldom or, more accurately, never overlooked. "He is like a
whirlwind," "She never sits still for one minute," "She keeps the
other children upset," "He's driving me up the wall" are comments that are often used to describe the child who is constantly
talking and on the go in the classroom. Even though the behavior
may rarely occur, hyperactive students can sit down, however.
They can look at books. They never talk one hundred percent of
the time. In other words, the desired behaviors are in the reper-
toire of the child, but they are seldom performed.

To minimize hyperactive behavior, use of a shaping procedure is essential and the steps must be small. If the terminal goal is to have the student sit without talking and look at a book for fifteen minutes, even one minute of the desired behavior may be too much to require initially. Perhaps thirty seconds would be more realistic. When the student has learned to sit still for thirty seconds, the length of time required before a reinforcer is delivered can be lengthened. It is better to go slowly with the process. A very gradual increase in the sitting and attending time required for a reward will increase the probability of success. The reinforcer for a hyperactive student will also need to be carefully chosen. Teacher praise and attention alone may be insufficient reinforcement. A tangible reward such as candy may also be required.

Summary

This chapter has stressed the importance of rewarding desirable student behavior as well as the conditions under which reinforcers should be delivered. Methods for selecting reinforcers were discussed and a number of potential classroom reinforcers were identified. Teacher attention was suggested as a viable reinforcer for most students. The possible reactions of different students, ideas for offering meaningful teacher approval, and alternative reinforcers are also explored. We pointed out that positive reinforcement that is applied indiscriminately will seldom produce the desired results. In order to use reinforcers effectively, teachers should: (1) specify the behavior to be increased (or decreased), (2) deliver contingent reinforcement, (3) reinforce immediately, (4) use frequent reinforcement to establish a behavior and intermittent reinforcement to maintain it, and (5) develop consistency in the kinds of behaviors that are reinforced. Strategies for strengthening the academic and social skills of students who seldom spontaneously emit desired responses was covered.

Focusing on desirable student behaviors, rather than emphasizing the negative aspects of their performance, can exert a powerful influence on the emotional climate in the classroom. A positive outlook is contagious. Classroom management problems are minimized when a teacher looks for the best in each student.

Suggested Projects

1. Undertake a program to increase the amount of approval you give students. You might want to begin by recording the number of positive and negative statements that you make each day. You could concentrate on increasing the approval you give to one or two students and measure any changes in their behavior.

2. If you are already giving considerable approval to the students, you might wish to consider new ways of showing approval. For example, you might develop a list of all the verbal statements you could use in expressing approval. You could also develop different strategies for delivering nonverbal approval. You might also find it helpful to log the reactions of the students to different forms of approval.

3. Talk with colleagues or even visit other schools to determine the reinforcers, other than teacher approval, that are being used to motivate students. Possibly visiting a setting where a token economy is being used would be beneficial.

4. List students' behaviors that never or seldom occur in the classroom, but that you would like to have occur frequently. Observe the students to determine if the behaviors occur occasionally. If they never occur, determine which initial elements of the desired behavior are present in the current behavior of the students. Plan a behavior-shaping program, beginning by reinforcing these elements. Gradually require more close approximations of the terminal behavior until the final goal is reached. If the students occasionally exhibit the desired behavior, initiate a systematic plan to reward the desired behavior.

REFERENCES

Kazdin, A. E. *Behavior modification in applied settings.* Homewood, Ill.: The Dorsey Press, 1975.

Krumboltz, J. D., and Krumboltz, H. B. *Changing children's behavior.* Englewood Cliffs, N.J.: Prentice-Hall, Inc., 1972.

Long, J. D., and Williams, R. L. *Classroom management with adolescents.* New York: MSS Information Corporation, 1973.

Neisworth, J. T.; Deno, S. L.; and Jenkins, J. R. *Student motivation and classroom management: A behavioristic approach.* Newark: Behavior Technics, Inc., 1969.

O'Leary, K. D. and O'Leary, S. G. *Classroom management: The successful use of behavior modification.* New York: Pergamon Press, Inc., 1972.

Piper, T. *Classroom management and behavioral objectives.* Belmont: Lear Siegler, Inc./ Fearon Publishers, 1974.

Williams, R. L. and Anandam, K. *Cooperative classroom management.* Columbus, Ohio: Charles E. Merrill Publishing Company, 1973.

Wilson, H. D., and Williams, R. L. *Before the geraniums die: A primer for classroom management.* New York: MSS Information Corporation, 1973.

CHAPTER FIVE

MANAGING
DISRUPTIVE BEHAVIOR

Exhibiting positive attitudes towards self and others, setting the stage for desirable behaviors, and reinforcing the occurrence of desirable behaviors can go a long way in minimizing disciplinary worries. Problems will still occur, however. Even the most amiable, astute disciplinarian cannot prevent every problem, because some events that precipitate problems are beyond the *immediate* and *total* control of the teacher. Unusual situations at home, occurrences in other classes, and interactions among students, for example, can set discipline problems in motion. But irrespective of the source, teachers must know how to handle problems when they do arise. Otherwise, problems will intensify and the classroom environment can become intolerable for the teacher and the students.

The most noticeable problems are usually disruptive in nature. Fighting, arguing, excessive noise making, shouting, disobedience, clowning around, and a host of other overt acts that distract attention and interrupt learning activities could be classified as disruptive. This chapter focuses on strategies for managing these and similar disruptive acts. You will notice that some of the strategies used in setting the stage for desirable behaviors can also be used to manage unwanted actions. Specifically, this chapter contains a number of positive as well as punitive alternatives for eliminating and reducing disruptive behaviors. The positive strategies include: altering setting events, reinforcing behaviors incompatible with disruptiveness, using peers as models, stimulus satiation, and extinction. The punitive strategies include: soft reprimands, time out, response cost, and overcorrection.

Altering Setting Events

Before you try more complicated strategies, you undoubtedly will want to think about possible changes in setting events (i.e., stimuli) that could reduce disruptive behaviors in your classroom. This strategy is one of the quickest and simplest ways of reducing problems. Its use involves only the identification and alteration of the events that seem to stimulate the undesirable behavior. The changes need not be drastic in order to be effective. Sometimes a very small change is all that is required to resolve a problem, e.g., temporarily separating two talkative students. Similarly, reducing the distance between yourself and a misbehaving student, changing the materials students are using, or altering the classroom routine may produce desired changes in behavior.

In making any changes, you will want to create as little fanfare as possible. Too much attention to a problem could instigate more of a disturbance than the one you hope to eliminate. For example, in separating two misbehaving students, you might quietly comment to the students involved, "I think it would be best for you to be seated in different areas today. That way both of you can get more accomplished." There is no reason to dwell on the misbehavior. Likewise, in moving closer to a misbehaving student, you should avoid any threatening gestures or statements that could generate a more serious problem. The idea is to let the misbehaving student know you are aware of the misbehavior and desire a change. Closer proximity paired with a nod towards the students' work should be sufficient in many instances. Changing texts or altering the routine can also be achieved without a lot of commotion from the teacher.

DEFUSING TENSE SITUATIONS

Mr. Carpenter was a seventh grade teacher who especially disliked aggressive behaviors. He could not tolerate one student's bullying another. Whenever he saw any sign of aggression, such as one student picking on another, he was quick to step in and admonish the aggressor. Mr. Carpenter's approach often generated more problems than it solved. The admonished student usually tried to get even with the other student during recess. And sometimes Mr. Carpenter made errors about who was at fault. Errors on his part typically led to disagreements and backtalk from wrongly accused students.

Mr. Carpenter realized something was wrong with his approach. He knew that temporarily separating talkative students was a useful way of reducing disturbances. So, he thought about how he could use changes in setting events to defuse situations among students. Mr. Carpenter decided that when he saw friction building up between two students he would remove one of the students from the setting. To avoid calling unnecessary attention to the problem, he simply would ask one of the students to run an errand or perform a chore for him. This tactic allowed both students time to "cool off" without providing any need for either to get even. Since aggressive acts for any particular student were infrequent, Mr. Carpenter did not have to worry about reinforcing aggression by letting a student perform a favor for him.

You have probably recognized that changing setting events would be effective with less serious disturbances or for preventing minor problems from spreading. But whether the changes you make are for preventing or for the solution of an existing problem, the strategy can be effective in reducing disturbances. One thing to remember in making changes in setting events is that a problem may reappear once you return to the original condition (e.g., when talkative students return to their regular seats). For that reason, you may need to combine stimulus

EVALUATION CHECKLIST FOR ALTERING SETTING EVENTS

Did you remember to:	Yes	No	Results and Recommendations
1. look for environmental factors that might be changed, e.g.: A. seating arrangements? B. proximity to chalkboard? C. proximity to teacher's desk? D. lighting? E. textbooks? F. other classroom materials? G. classroom routine (roll-taking, administrative duties)? H. method of lesson presentation? I. other?			
2. make changes quietly in order not to create a greater disturbance?			
3. combine the use of altering setting events with other strategies?			

changes with other strategies. For example, after you make a change in setting events, you could reinforce the appearance of desired behaviors. Some experimenting should help you determine what works best for you and your students.

Reinforcing Behaviors Incompatible with Disruptiveness

Another strategy for reducing a disruptive behavior is to reinforce behavior incompatible with that response. When one behavior is incompatible with another, the two cannot occur simultaneously. For example, a student cannot be aggressive and cooperative at the same time. Similarly, students cannot simultaneously talk and listen, agree and disagree, stand and sit, or be tardy and on time. So, once you have identified the behaviors you want reduced, your task is to strengthen the opposite of those behaviors. Strengthening an incompatible behavior will lead automatically to a reduction in the other behavior. Unfortunately, teachers sometimes get so involved with dealing directly with disruptive behavior that they forget about strategies that will resolve problems indirectly.

Although the reinforcement of incompatible behavior sounds easy (and often is), several factors that could pose problems deserve careful consideration. First, a few students may exhibit only minimal amounts of the behaviors you wish to strengthen. An aggressive student, for instance, may engage in few cooperative acts. In such instances you would need to shape the desired behavior. That is, you would need initially to reinforce any sign of cooperation. The requirements for reinforcement would then be increased gradually as you moved towards the terminal goal—greater cooperation and less aggression. Second, in strengthening incompatible behaviors you must use reinforcers that are meaningful to the students, otherwise you will have little success in producing wanted changes. What is reinforcing to some students could have minimal influence on others. Social attention (e.g., praise) may be adequate for some students. For others, you may have to rely upon tangibles, tokens, activities, or intangibles. The key to success, however, will depend largely upon making the desired behaviors pay off for the students. You cannot get what is not paid for.

A general application. A study by Allyon and Roberts (1974) clearly demonstrates the benefits of reinforcing incompatible behaviors. These researchers were interested in reducing negative behaviors among five of the most disruptive students in a large fifth grade reading class (thirty-eight students). The average level of such behavior among the most disruptive students was 34 percent, while these students' correct responses on daily reading assignments was below 50 percent. The disruptions included such acts as running, walking around the room, loud talking, noise making, and a variety of other overt acts. Instead of trying to reduce these behaviors directly through punishment and other means, a token economy was established. The system enabled students to earn points for completing academic assignments. Students could earn two points for 80 percent accuracy on an assignment and five points for 100 percent accuracy. The points could be cashed in daily or weekly for a variety of back-up reinforcers. For example, two points would buy fifteen minutes access to a game room or ten minutes of extra recess. Reduced detention, becoming an assistant teacher, and having free time to work on a bulletin board were a few of the other back-up reinforcers that could be purchased.

The results were highly encouraging. By the end of the study, the average rate of accuracy on academic performances for the five most disruptive students rose to about 85 percent. And although no direct effort was made to reduce disruptiveness, the average rate of disruptive behavior fell to about 5 percent. Apparently,the kinds of behaviors being reinforced were incompatible with disruptiveness. Students were reportedly heard making such remarks as "Shut up, I'm trying to do my work," and "Quit bugging me, can't you see I'm reading?"

Using Peers as Models

Modeling, like positive reinforcement, is a strategy that has broad applications in the classroom. Chapter Three showed how the strategy could be used to prompt desired student behavior. Emphasis there was on ways in which the teacher could serve as a model. In this section, you will briefly examine how modeling can be used to reduce unwanted responses. Emphasis here will be on pointing out appropriate models among the students.

You undoubtedly realize that students learn much of their behavior simply by observing and imitating that of their peers. Your realization of this fact can be helpful because you can draw attention to the kinds of behavior worthy of imitation. Suppose that John and Frank are talking when they should be working on a classroom assignment. Instead of calling attention to their disruptive behavior, you might choose to let them hear you tell Bill, "I'm glad to see you working so quietly on your assignment. Keep up the good work." Your approving comment will enable John and Frank to see the kind of behavior that produces approval. This strategy is especially useful since you need not wait for the misbehaving students to exhibit praiseworthy responses; you can identify and direct attention to the appropriate behavior being exhibited by someone else. Of course, you want to be certain to reinforce the disruptive student or students should they elect to imitate the desired behavior. Broden et al. (1970), in fact, have found that reinforcing the attending behavior of one student increased not only that behavior but also that of a disruptive student in an adjacent seat. It is hoped that you will also obtain changes in disruptive behaviors by drawing attention to the appropriate behavior of others.

INAPPROPRIATE USE OF A MODEL

Mrs. Morris, a tenth grade English teacher, was an avid reader. She eagerly consumed practically every new book on the market; a best seller never escaped her attention. She loved to discuss the books she read with the students. The problem was that only one of Mrs. Morris's students, Steve, enjoyed reading as much as she. Mrs. Morris found herself directing more of her attention towards Steve. She would comment, "I'll bet Steve has read this book. Why not let him give his views." Invariably, he had read the book. Steve became the one student that Mrs. Morris wanted others to emulate. She often used him as an example and said more than once "I wish more of you could be like Steve." How do you think others felt about Steve? About Mrs. Morris?

You no doubt recognized from the preceding example the major problem of using students as role models: students can become jealous when a classmate is held up as an example, and becomes the exclusive recipient of teacher attention. That student may then be labeled as "teacher's pet" and receive considerable ridicule from others. You can avoid such an occurrence by occasionally using every student as a role model. Even the most disruptive student will exhibit some behavior worthy of recognition. Also, by drawing attention to appropriate behavior of models, you can avoid making comparisons with other students. Saying, "I wish others could be like . . ." can only generate jealousy and resentment. A better strategy is to call attention to the desired behavior without putting others down. It is sufficient to say "I like the way John is . . . ."

Successful use of models, however, will depend on more than appropriately recognizing desirable behaviors of your students. As you will recall from Chapter Three, the teacher who is prestigious, in some way similar to the students, positive in treatment of students, and who presents tasks in an uncomplicated manner is likely to be frequently imitated. The same is generally true with student models. Students who have status with observers, are similar to the observers (e.g., in age, sex, background, or interests), and who obtain positive results from their behavior are more likely to be imitated than models who lack status, are dissimilar, and do not get reinforced for their behavior. You will recognize from the above comments that the consequences for imitating the behavior of a model are also of critical importance. Unless an individual is positively reinforced for imitative behavior, that behavior is unlikely to persist for very long. So, your use of student examples will have to be closely tied to your use of positive reinforcement. A combination of the two strategies should vastly improve class behavior.

Using Stimulus Satiation

Satiation is yet another non-punitive strategy that can be used to reduce disruptive behavior. You are probably familiar with the strategy from your own personal experiences. Do you recall spending so much time with a good friend that the friendship waned? Or eating so many sundaes that you became sick of those treats? The same thing can happen with classroom behaviors. You can ask students to repeat an undesirable behavior until they tire of (i.e., satiate) it.

An interesting example reported by Allyon (1963) should clarify how satiation can alter unwanted behaviors. He used the strategy to eliminate the excessive towel-hoarding by a mental patient. The patient usually had from twenty to thirty towels in her room every day. During satiation, Allyon asked nurses to deliver rather than remove towels from the patient's room. They delivered about seven towels each day during the first week and about sixty towels each day by the third week. During the first week, the patient seemed to love the new procedure. She was frequently seen fondling the towels, and expressed appreciation for the kindness of the nurses. After two weeks, however, the patient was requesting that no more towels be delivered, and at the end of the sixth week she was removing towels herself. She simply had had enough of a "good thing."

Teachers, too, report successful use of satiation. Familiar examples to all of us include having students blow gum bubbles, whistle, and sail paper airplanes until the novelty and reinforcement of those acts wear off. The strategy might also work for reducing profanity (done in private, of course), finger snapping, singing, or any behavior that can be readily repeated. The behavior simply needs to be repeated until it is no longer reinforcing. What starts out as being humorous can lose much of its appeal with repetition.

While satiation can be a viable alternative to punishing a student or ordering a student *not* to do something, the strategy has its hazards. First, a student may be unwilling to emit the undesirable behavior repeatedly. Satiation can work only if you get a student to perform. Second, if the student does not tire of whatever makes the behavior reinforcing, then the unwanted behavior could become more firmly established as a result of the extra practice. It is usually best, therefore, to get a few repetitions beyond the point where the student first indicates a desire to terminate the act. This extra effort should ensure that satiation does occur.

Extinction

You learned in Chapter Four that the use of reinforcement strengthens behavior and thus increases the probability of the behavior's occurring again. It was also mentioned that both desirable and undesirable behavior can be strengthened by the payoff they produce. The reverse is also true. Behaviors strengthened by reinforcement can be weakened when reinforcement is withheld. The strategy of withholding reinforcement is called extinction. While many possible reinforcers can be withheld to alter different responses, attention is generally the reinforcer withheld to weaken undesirable behavior in classroom settings. Our discussion of extinction will therefore focus on how behaviors can be weakened by withholding social attention.

Withholding Teacher Attention

Teachers are sometimes heard to comment, "That student is just misbehaving to get my attention." Such a statement indicates they are aware of the pervasive influence of their attention. Unfortunately, teachers frequently continue delivering exactly what the student is trying to produce—teacher attention. In other words, they recognize what the student is trying to get with misbehavior, but then fail to do what is needed for producing change. Students will continue emitting responses that pay off. And the payoff in terms of attention need not be positive. Students who do not get attention for desired behaviors may find any form of attention to be reinforcing. Besides, being fussed at might help a student get out of doing an assignment, gain the attention of peers, or let him know he has the teachers irritated. Students can make a game out of getting the teacher mad.

An interesting study (Madsen, Becker, Thomas, Koser, and Plager, 1968) supporting the value of withholding attention for excessive amounts of unwanted behaviors showed that the more teachers told students to sit down, the more the students stood up. In that classroom, students were receiving little attention for sitting and working, and so the attention for standing, although in the form of reprimands, served to reinforce out-of-seat behavior. When teachers quit telling the students to sit down and instead started praising sitting and working, the students spent more time in their seats, working. Other studies have demonstrated that withholding attention can be a helpful addition to reducing argumentative statements (Hall, et al., 1971), tantrums (Zimmerman and Zimmerman, 1962), hyperactivity (Patterson, 1965), aggression (Brown and Elliot, 1965), and disruptiveness (Becker, Madsen, Arnold, and Thomas, 1967; Kazdin, 1973). Seldom, however, is withholding of adult attention the sole strategy for producing behavioral changes. Praise or other reinforcers for desired behaviors are typically paired with the withholding of attention for undesirable behavior. In fact, studies (e.g., Madsen, Becker, and Thomas, 1968) have indicated that merely ignoring inappropriate behavior without the use of other strategies could lead to increases in inappropriate behavior. Nonetheless, the literature clearly suggests that teachers should avoid "catching" students in every deviant act. To do so would only serve to increase misbehavior. Successful classroom management involves the teacher's being able to overlook some problems.

Apparently, teachers cannot ignore every deviant act that occurs in the classroom. To avoid giving attention to some responses would be catastropic. When students might injure themselves or others, for example, the teacher should respond quickly. Also, when disruptive responses occur repeatedly, teachers cannot simply turn their heads and expect the problem to disappear. Such a tactic would be naive, to say the least. We shall discuss later ways in which serious, frequently occurring problems can be managed. The point now is that certain behaviors can be overlooked in order to weaken them and diminish their immediate impact. For example, students who snap their fingers to get the teacher's attention, or call out answers without raising their hands can be ignored. If the teacher recognizes only students who raise their hands, *everyone* may soon get the idea of what is required. No big issue will have been created and no unnecessary embarrassment will have resulted for the students. Similarly, teachers can avoid responding when students occasionally make a "cute" remark or an argumentative statement. Walking away will let the student know the teacher does not have to get in the last word. Furthermore, the student will have been deprived of an opportunity to practice becoming a better arguer. Whining, pouting, complaining, and excessive verbalizing would be other student behaviors that could easily be put on extinction. Students will eventually stop emitting behaviors that do not pay off. Life will also be more pleasant for the teacher who realizes that a 100 percent detection rate on misbehavior is unnecessary for establishing effective classroom management.

SEEKING ATTENTION
Billy was a third grader who had lots of things to tell his teacher, Mrs. Martin. Whenever he saw anything wrong in the classroom, he would call her aside to let her know what was happening. He usually made at least twenty to thirty trips to her desk every day to keep her informed. He made other visits to ask for special help and to find out "exactly" what he was supposed to be doing. Any hurt also sent him clamoring for Mrs. Martin. She was so exasperated from the other attention given to Billy that she seldom gave Billy any attention when he was cooperating with others, working on his assignments, or simply minding his own business. What would you recommend?

Withholding attention for undesirable behavior has broad applications in the classroom. But certain factors should be considered if the strategy is to be properly used. First, teachers must remain consistent in what they will and will not attend to. Ignoring a behavior one day and calling attention to it the next will strengthen, rather than weaken, it. Students will learn that the payoff will eventually be delivered if they are persistent enough. A good tactic for teachers would be to make a list of the behaviors they will reinforce, as well as a list of those to be ignored. Having clear objectives in mind should produce greater consistency. Second, teachers should be prepared for a possible increase in undesirable behavior when attention for those behaviors is withheld. Individuals who have been accustomed to getting something for their misbehavior will probably "try harder" when the payoffs are no longer forthcoming. However, if reinforcement is available for other responses, students will soon learn what behaviors pay off. Third, teachers should realize that withholding their attention will weaken undesirable behavior only if *their attention* is the actual reinforcer for the undesirable behavior. It may well be that other events are maintaining the unwanted behaviors. The real test comes from consistently withholding attention and evaluating the results. In many instances, a teacher might ignore student behaviors only to have those behaviors reinforced by a student's peers. Ignoring the "class clowns," for instance, would be ineffective as long as classmates laugh and otherwise support undesirable antics. Because peers can provide attention for behaviors the teacher may be trying to extinguish, we need to take a look at how teachers might enlist the help of students.

Obtaining the Cooperation of Peers

Most teachers would agree that peer attention is a powerful influence in the development of both desirable and undesirable student behavior, but teachers have sometimes been remiss in mobilizing peer attention. Perhaps the conception that teachers *alone* should manage class affairs has hindered seeking the support of students. Nonetheless, for those who desire the cooperation of students, several possibilities exist for getting students to use their attention in ways that benefit others.

First, teachers can plan classroom discussions to help students recognize the importance of peer attention. During class discussions, teachers might ask; "Why do some students break class rules although it only seems to get them into trouble? What would happen if no one paid attention when individuals engaged in disruptive activities? How can classmates help others make greater academic progress?" At least a few, if not all, students will surmise that peer attention often sustains undesirable acts, that peers withholding their attention could weaken those behaviors, and that peer approval for appropriate behaviors could have favorable impact on the entire class. Periodic discussions could very well sharpen everyone's understanding of why people behave as they do. Some disruptive youngsters might alter their own behaviors after they see what is sustaining their actions. Further, teachers could use these discussions to solicit the cooperation of students.

It would probably be best for teachers to avoid having discussions about disruptiveness immediately following an unpleasant classroom incident. There is no reason to embarrass anyone. A better strategy would be to select a time when no disruptive acts have recently occurred. Possibly, discussions could be held when class rules are being established. Or, if the teacher has a time set aside for discussing class activities with students, that time would be appropriate. Establishing a cooperative planning time, or setting aside a time, say, every grading period, to discuss student and teacher concerns would be an appropriate step for teachers at any grade level.

Another possibility for obtaining peer cooperation in ignoring inappropriate behaviors would be initially to seek support from those students who appear to have the most potential for influencing others. Solomon and Wahler (1973) conducted an experiment that demonstrated the utility of this approach. They selected peer "therapists" who had shown a willingness to cooperate with adults and who were also popular with their sixth grade classmates. They received training in spotting desirable and problem behaviors via video tape. They also heard explanations about extinction and reinforcement procedures. They were asked later to ignore problem behaviors among disruptive classmates and to respond positively to desirable behaviors. The results were encouraging. During experimental conditions, the "therapists" gave less attention to problem behavior. Those behaviors among disruptive classmates decreased substantially. The peers were not as successful in responding positively to desirable behaviors. Perhaps longer periods of training were required for responding positively than merely for ignoring others' actions. But the study showed that teachers can get selected students to help produce needed changes. This tactic might be required in classes where the teacher cannot rely upon the help of all students. The support of larger numbers of students could be sought after the teacher has achieved success with selected groups.

Whether teachers are working with an entire class or with a small group, an effort should be made to reinforce students for judiciously using their attention. Teacher approval would be a potential reinforcer for most students. Special privileges, tangibles, or tokens might also be considered. Long and Williams (1973) have demonstrated, too, that group rewards are useful in getting students to attend appropriately to the behavior of others. When a reward is contingent upon the desirable behavior of *every* student, peers are reluctant to support undesirable behaviors. However, when teachers choose to use group rewards, they should be sure every student can perform the expected behaviors. Furthermore, if one or two students fail to respond to group payoffs, the strategy should be altered so that others are not continuously deprived of privileges because of a few students.

Evaluating Your Use of Reinforcement Techniques

Reinforcement techniques represent effective methods for reducing disruptive behavior in the classroom. The evaluation checklist on pages 88-89 can be useful in determining whether the techniques have been properly implemented.

Punishment

Although the positive strategies described above can have far-reaching effects on student behaviors, situations may arise occasionally when punishment is required to suppress an undesirable behavior immediately. A student who may do harm to himself or others requires immediate attention. Similarly, if a student has failed to respond to positive strategies, the teacher cannot indefinitely overlook repeated instances of misbehavior. Action is required to keep the student and others from assuming that the undesirable behavior is permissible. But even in isolated cases, where behavior necessitates the use of punishment, the type of punishment must be carefully selected and used with discretion. Otherwise, the teacher could create more problems than will be resolved by the punishment.

EVALUATION CHECKLIST FOR REINFORCEMENT TECHNIQUES
TO REDUCE INAPPROPRIATE BEHAVIOR

Did you remember to:	Yes	No	Results and Recommendations

1. focus on behavior you would like to increase by:
  A. identifying behaviors that are incompatible with inappropriate behavior?
  B. reinforcing the behaviors that are incompatible with the inappropriate behaviors?
  C. shaping the desired behaviors by initially reinforcing approximations of the terminal goal behavior?			

2. use peers as models appropriately by:
  A. directing attention to desired behavior through comments to students who exhibit the behavior?
  B. occasionally using every student as a role model?
  C. avoiding making comparisons between students?
  D. combining reinforcement of appropriate behavior with peer modeling?			

3. consider whether you can induce satiation of harmless behaviors (e.g., humming, finger snapping)?			
4. withhold attention from inappropriate behaviors?			
5. remain consistent in the behaviors you reinforce?			
6. determine whether teacher or peer attention is maintaining the inappropriate behavior?			
7. reduce peer attention to inappropriate behavior by: A. talking with the students about the importance of ignoring inappropriate behavior?			

EVALUATION CHECKLIST FOR REINFORCEMENT TECHNIQUES
(continued)

Did you remember to:	Yes	No	Results and Recommendations
B. identifying potentially influential students who will cooperate in ignoring peer deviancy?			
C. reinforcing students for ignoring inappropriate behaviors?			

Types of Punishment

Many persons think of only one form of punishment when the need for quick action arises. They usually think of applying an aversive or negative stimulus to the "culprit." This is typically referred to as type 1 punishment. Paddlings and harsh criticism (e.g., loud reprimands, criticism directed at the person) qualify as aversive for *most* students and thus their use would be examples of type 1 punishment.

A MISTAKEN "PUNISHER"

Mr. Edwards relied heavily upon corporal punishment in disciplining boys in his eighth grade class. It was not uncommon for him to line up five or six boys and give every one of them a "good thrashing." The boys would howl, rub their behinds, and generally "horse around" before and after each took his licks. Mr. Edwards noticed that the boys did not really seem to mind the paddlings. Oddly enough, they seemed to enjoy them. He also noticed that the paddlings were ineffective in changing the boys' behaviors. One day after lunch, he accidentally discovered why the paddlings were so ineffective. The boys were lined up trading licks. They were making a game of being able to take hard licks with a wooden paddle. One student even commented, "You can't even hit as hard as Edwards." He realized that what appeared to be punishment was not punishing at all for these boys. He resolved to try something else.

The preceding example may be atypical, but occasionally teachers will use what they think is a harsh punisher only to find that their perceptions do not fit the students' perceptions. Real punishers suppress behaviors. Although paddlings, harsh criticism, and similar acts may temporarily suppress unwanted behaviors for most students, we must still caution against their use for several reasons. First, these punishers generally place the teacher in the role of an aggressive model. Teachers who manage their frustrations by physically (or verbally) striking out at students run the risk of teaching students to deal with their frustrations in a similar fashion. It is indeed paradoxical that a teacher would try to suppress fighting among students through the use of corporal punishment. Second, these punishers may generate any number of emotional reactions from the students. For example, students may counterattack. We do not know how many personal assaults on teachers actually follow teacher attacks on students. Perhaps none. Nevertheless, assaults on teachers and vandalism in the schools are on the increase (*The New York Times,* 1976). One can only speculate why students attack teachers and return to school at night to break windows, set fires, and write on school walls. Part of the answer may be a result of the kind of punishment that students received. Physical punishment and harsh criticism may have just the opposite emotional influence on some students. Some students may feel so threatened and intimidated that they are afraid to do much of anything. Furthermore, the more timid students who observe others being punished may become so upset that they become less productive. Other students may simply choose to remain at home. Much of the absenteeism and tardiness in the schools could be an effort to avoid the aversive tactics used at school. Third, the choice of physical punishment or a similar approach could become so upsetting to the teacher that he cannot function for the rest of the day (or longer). "This hurts me worse than you" is frequently more than hollow verbage. Finally, physical punishment and harsh criticism do little to engender a love of learning. For these and other reasons (e.g., legal problems), teachers are well advised to look for other means of suppressing unwanted behaviors.

An alternative to type 1 punishment consists of withdrawing positive reinforcers.[1] This approach is known as type 2 punishment. Examples are: (1) *time out,* involves the temporary removal

---

[1]You will recognize a fine distinction between extinction and type 2 punishment. With extinction, when an undesirable behavior occurs, reinforcers are simply withheld for that behavior. With type 2 punishment, a reinforcer is actually *taken away,* that is, the person being punished gives up something of value. For example, with time out, the disruptor is taken away (all potential reinforcers are given up) and with response cost the person forfeits token, privileges, etc.

of the opportunity for any reinforcement; (2) *response cost,* the withdrawal of reinforcing consequences such as tokens, free time, or special privileges; and (3) *overcorrection,* [2] removal of probable sources of reinforcement when disruptors are required to correct their disruptions immediately. The use of type 2 punishers are generally more acceptable to teachers because they minimize the likelihood of adverse side effects. For example, they eliminate the provision of an aggressive model for students to imitate. Counterattacks should also be less likely, since no aversive stimulus is presented to the students. Indeed, the overall strategy of removing positive reinforcers should minimize the adverse emotional reaction associated with the use of certain type 1 punishers. No form of punishment is entirely pleasant, however, and if it were, students would be unaffected by its use. The idea is to let students know their inappropriate behaviors do not pay without, at the same time, turning students against school. Rather than removing all the unpleasantness of punishment, teachers should concentrate on how to use properly the punishers they select. Inappropriate use of any tactic can create problems. Let us look now at a few major guidelines that may help you use punishment more judiciously.

The Effective Use of Punishment

In Chapter Four, we discussed a number of factors that influence the effective use of positive reinforcement. Similar factors influence the effective use of punishment. First, behaviors that may result in punishment should be clearly specified. As we have suggested previously, students sometimes unwittingly get themselves into trouble. They break a rule and then are told about the rule. Letting students know what is appropriate and inappropriate should reduce the necessity for using punishment. Most students will behave appropriately if they know what is expected of them. Furthermore, clearly specifying what behaviors will result in punishment can be extremely helpful to the teacher. Teachers who know what actions they plan to take with different behaviors should be less likely to

---

[2]We have chosen to classify overcorrection as a type 2 punisher because the strategy involves potential forfeitures of reinforcers. One could argue, however, that correction of disturbances is the application of an aversive stimulus. You can choose how you view overcorrection after you have had a chance to study the strategy later in the chapter.

punish indiscriminately. Certain behaviors, although undesirable, and perhaps very irritating to teachers, should never be punished. For example, shyness and timidity suggest that students need help in acquiring desired responses. Students should not be punished for these responses.

Second, once the behaviors that lead to punishment have been identified, punishment should be delivered contingent upon the occurrence of *those* behaviors. And, when delivering the punishment, the teacher should tell misbehaving students what they are being punished for so they can see the contingent relationship between the undesirable behavior and its consequences. Before the teacher delivers punishment, however, he will want to issue at least one warning. The warning itself could reduce the need for punishment. But, if the warning is insufficient, punishment should be forthcoming. Students who learn that certain behaviors lead to punishment may be willing to forego engaging in those behaviors. Third, punishment should closely follow the undesirable behavior. Delay in delivering punishment could result in the misbehaving student's failing to see the relationship between the undesirable behavior and its consequences. Research (Walter, Park, and Cane, 1965) has also shown that punishment that is introduced early in a response sequence (e.g., when the misbehavior is just beginning) is more effective than punishment introduced later in a response sequence. Waiting until misbehavior has spread to others before action is taken may also increase the necessity for using punishment with others.

Fourth, we mentioned in the previous chapter that the establishment of a new response is facilitated when the response is reinforced each time it occurs. Suppression of a response calls for punishment *each* time the response occurs. Behaviors that reliably produce punishment are less likely to be emitted than behaviors that produce reinforcement. Fifth, a point closely related to the preceding one is the need for teachers to be consistent in what they do. The teacher who overlooks a behavior one day and punishes the same behavior the next may only confuse students. Similarly, the teacher who is inconsistent in following through on threats may cause students to conclude "She is only bluffing," or "He won't do anything to you." Sixth, the amount of intensity of punishment can influence the effectiveness of punishment (Parke and Walters, 1967; Solomon, 1964). Generally speaking, the more intense the punishment, the longer lasting the effect. This does *not* mean that teachers should use extremely aversive strategies. Mildly aversive stimuli may be sufficiently intense to supress undesirable classroom behaviors. The teacher needs only to use punishers that are sufficiently aversive to suppress the unwanted behaviors. Finally, as with positive reinforcers, the teacher must realize that what is punishing to one student may not be punishing to another student or even the same student every time it is used. Students can become satiated with a punisher the same way they can with a given reward. This fact is yet another reason to preclude ever using any single approach.

Now that we have these general guidelines behind us, let us look at a few of specific punishers that seem most appropriate for classroom teachers.

Soft Reprimands

One form of type 1 punishment that appears effective in reducing disruptive behavior without producing adverse side effects is the use of soft reprimands. Several studies (O'Leary and Becker, 1968; O'Leary, Kaufman, Kass, and Drabman, 1970) show that soft reprimands, audible only to the misbehaving student, are more effective than loud reprimands in reducing disruptive classroom behaviors. O'Leary, et. al. (1970) note that soft reprimands have at least three advantages over loud ones. First, they do not call the attention of the entire class to the misbehavior. You will recall from earlier discussions that too much attention to inappropriate behavior could serve as a reinforcer for that behavior. Second, since soft reprimands may be different from what disruptive youngsters customarily receive at home or at school, they should be less likely to trigger emotional reactions. A youngster who receives harsh treatment at home is certainly entitled to different treatment from teachers. Third, soft reprimands may represent an acceptable alternative for teachers. We know of *no* teachers who never disapprove of student behavior. We know of many teachers, though, who wish they had explored alternative ways of expressing their disapproval. Soft reprimands are surely superior to sarcasm and shouts.

DID I SAY THAT?

Mrs. Craven's first graders sometimes got too noisy with their work. To quiet them, she would try talking louder than the students. She got so accustomed to talking over the students that she did not even realize how loudly she was talking. Sometimes she practically shouted orders to the students. She did not even consider what she was saying.

One day as part of an assignment for a graduate class she was taking, Mrs. Craven made a recording of her own teaching. She could not believe what she heard. She was shouting, "Please get quiet!" "Get back to work!" "Don't you know better than that?" Fortunately, after making the discovery about herself, Mrs. Craven decided she wanted to respond differently to her students.

As with all punitive strategies, soft reprimands must be used cautiously. Teachers must be careful about how frequently they use reprimands. The need to rely heavily on any form of disapproval suggests something is fundamentally wrong. Perhaps the instructional program needs revision, or the teacher may need to examine whether students are being reinforced for desirable behaviors. Teachers must also be cautious about *what* is being reprimanded. Disapproval should always be directed at behavior. The students themselves should never be the targets of disapproval. Personal attacks on the students can lower their self-concepts. Comments such as "Don't you have any respect for the rights of others?" or "I should have expected that from you" make unneeded implications about the *person*. Furthermore, affronts on the students are frequently associated with counterattacks. Most students can accept mild reproof for their behavior, but few students appreciate statements that go beyond what is needed to correct misbehavior. We should also caution against overdwelling on misbehavior. A soft reprimand that is short and to the point will be better received than a long oration. Reprimands that involve bringing up every past iniquity will overburden the students as well as unnecessarily take up class time. Stick with present offenses. Finally, we should point out that soft reprimands are most applicable when teachers can move freely about the class. Occasions may arise when teachers cannot immediately move close enough to a student to deliver a soft reprimand. In those instances, teachers can respond mildly (rather than shouting), direct disapproval at the behavior, and be brief in stating what is wrong and what should be done about it. Adhering to the guidelines provided earlier in the chapter for using punishment will also facilitate the appropriate use of soft reprimands.

Time Out

Another mild form of punishment that is especially suited for reducing disruptive behavior of kindergarten and elementary students is the time out procedure. The procedure typically involves removing the misbehaving student from the classroom for a brief time period, say, for five or ten minutes. The tactic of removing the student minimizes the opportunity of his receiving reinforcement for his misdeeds. The student who is no longer in a setting to receive peer and teacher attention should be less inclined to engage in disruptive acts. At times, the tactic will also give the teacher, as well as the student, a chance to cool off.

The usefulness of time out is illustrated in a study by LeBlanc, Busby, and Thomson (1974). The subject of the study was a four-year old boy enrolled in a preschool class with fifteen other children. He frequently made physical attacks on other children, called them names, and made demands to "Give me that" or "Shut up." Before time out was begun, the teachers repeatedly tried controlling the child by admonishing him for his aggression. This proved ineffective. Two types of time out were then implemented. The first step consisted of removing the youngster from the play area and placing him in a "time out chair." If he refused to go to the chair or left it before a minute was up without first obtaining permission, he was sent to a time out room. The time out strategies were used first in dealing with the physical attacks, then with the name calling, and finally with the inappropriate demands on other children. Each time the time out strategies were used with one of the aggressive behaviors, the behavior declined immediately to near zero. Soon, only the time out chair was needed and eventually that was no longer required.

In order for time out to be effective, several conditions must be present. First, the classroom from which the student is removed must be reinforcing. If the classroom is itself aversive, then it would be nonpunitive to remove the misbehaving student. The student might even consider time out to be the lesser of two evils. Second, the setting used for time out must be devoid of opportunities for reinforcement. Placing a student in a busy hallway, for example, would be unsuitable. Too much opportunity exists in the hall for the student to talk with others or obtain other reinforcements. The principal's office, nurse's room, and similar settings would be unacceptable for similar reasons. A more likely time out area would be an empty room adjacent to the classroom. Teachers sometimes turn a cloak room into a time out area. Other teachers have found that a portable partition placed in the back of the class is suitable. Any area that is selected should be well lighted and well ventilated. Time out is *not* intended to frighten the student. You will also want to remember that it should be of short duration. Ten minutes might be considered as an upper limit to exclude a student from the class. Occasionally even less time is required. You could try going to the student after a few minutes to ask if he is ready to return to the class and behave appropriately. This approach could reduce the amount of time the student is out of class. While a long stay from the class might do the teacher some good, students do not learn appropriate behavior by being excluded from activities. Further, when a student returns to class, the exile should end: the student should be reinforced for appropriate behaviors.

Although the preceding conditions can help make time out effective, you should be prepared for several potential problems in using time out. You will need to be prepared for the occasional student who refuses to go to the time out area. Under such circumstances, you will want to remain calm or else you could create more commotion than the student. Calmly reminding the student of the predetermined rule that X behavior leads to time out should be sufficient with most students. A few students may require more persuasion. You may have to ask the principal to escort the student to time out, or a conference with the student's parents may be required. Parents, of course, should be made aware of the strategies that you are using to manage disruptions. Surreptitious use of time out could lead to problems. Let parents know what you expect and how you plan to manage problems. Get their suggestions. Used infrequently and properly, time out can be an innocuous way of managing problem behaviors. Parents will probably agree once they know what you are doing and what you are trying to achieve.

Response Cost

A third alternative to harsh punishment·is response cost. This strategy is particularly suited to classes where token economies or special privileges are being used to enhance desired behaviors. Since rewards are being given for desired behaviors, fines and loss of privileges (costs) can readily be used to weaken unwanted behaviors. In fact, combining both rewards and response cost may assist students to learn more quickly that appropriate behaviors pay, while inappropriate ones do not. However, you will want to avoid relying so heavily upon response cost that students are reluctant to engage in any behavior for fear it will cost them.

I EARNED FIFTY DOLLARS AT SCHOOL TODAY

Mr. Padgett, a general business teacher, had read about token economies and the use of response cost, but he was skeptical of their usefulness. He decided to give tokens a try only after other strategies had failed to get students interested in his class. Disruptive behaviors were so frequent that he was even considering quitting.

Mr. Padgett began by having a student committee design and duplicate "money" to be used as tokens. He held a class discussion to determine how much should be paid for appropriate behaviors, lost for inappropriate behaviors, and how the money could be spent. The students (and Mr. Padgett) agreed that money could be earned for attendance, being on time, having appropriate materials, assignments completed (amount depended on accuracy), special projects, and participating in daily lesson activities. Fines (response cost) were imposed for disruptive behaviors such as loud talking, fighting, and destruction of school materials. Any earnings could be used to purchase free time, special privileges, and leadership roles in the class. The students rotated the responsibility for helping Mr. Padgett maintain accurate payroll records. He was surprised at the way students got involved in class activities. Grades improved and disruptive behaviors declined appreciably.

To use response cost effectively, you will need to limit the use of the procedure to highly disruptive behaviors. Imposing a fine or loss of privilege for every misdeed would generate unnecessary anxiety. Students must be free to make mistakes. Also, the price for engaging in an undesirable behavior should be reasonable. A student who has worked diligently all period to earn ten tokens should not lose his entire earnings because of a single inappropriate act. Loss of one or two tokens might be sufficient to inhibit the behavior. Whatever is withdrawn needs only to be costly enough to reduce the behavior in question. One group of researchers (Hall, Axelrod, Foundopoulos, Shellman, Campbell, and

Cranston, 1972) found that merely taking back colored slips of paper with the student's name on them each time he cried or complained was sufficient to reduce those behaviors. We should caution, however, that what is withdrawn should not be a privilege to which students are entitled by school policy. Withholding recess is a popular tactic in elementary schools, but this constitutes a misuse of response cost. The action is also illegal in many states. A better technique is to establish special rewards or privileges (e.g., free time) that are separate from the regular school activities. These can then be temporarily withheld whenever students fail to perform appropriately.

While response cost is an easy technique to use, it has its perils. Students may become upset when a privilege is withheld. You, of course, should remain calm about emotional reactions. A good strategy is to ignore the response and continue with classroom activities. Being fair in imposing the penalties with all misbehaving students will reduce complaints and emotional reactions from students. Indicating how students can redeem themselves may also prove helpful. You should also consider that a response such as "He'll penalize me again and see if I care" could be a signal that the student does indeed care about being penalized. If not, why the reaction? A second problem may arise when a student is repeatedly fined for a misbehavior. Some students may try to see how many tokens or privileges they can lose. This problem can be averted by setting an upper limit on the number of times response cost will be imposed before more severe actions are taken.

Overcorrection

A mildly punitive strategy recently tested by Foxx and Azrin (1972) holds considerable promise for reducing disruptive behaviors. The strategy requires that disruptive individuals restore the environment to a better condition than existed before their disruptiveness. Thus, the procedure is called overcorrection or restitution. Foxx and Azrin's initial use of the strategy eliminated several disruptive-aggressive behaviors of one brain-damaged and two mentally retarded patients. For example, one of the patients frequently damaged furniture by throwing and overturning beds, tables, and chairs. Disapproval of the actions and having the patient upright the overturned furniture was ineffective in reducing the undesirable behavior. When the overcorrection procedure was begun, the patient was required to restore the overturned furniture to its correct position and to straighten and clean all other furniture in the ward. Overcorrection resulted in an immediate reduction in the undesirable behavior and completely eliminated the long-standing behavior within twelve weeks.

Subsequent use of the strategy (Azrin and Wesolowski, 1974) proved effective in eliminating stealing among retarded adults. Overcorrection applied to stealing consisted of having the offender return more than was actually taken from the victim. If the offender stole food (e.g., a candy bar), he had to return the food plus an identical item. Previously, a simple correction procedure of having him return the stolen property was unsuccessful in reducing thievery. Once the stealing began costing the thief, however, it quickly ended. The overcorrection strategy also reversed the typical condition in which the victim is the one who suffers.

Overcorrection has also been used in treating autistic behaviors (Azrin, Kaplan, and Foxx, 1973) and bedwetting (Azrin, Sneed, and Foxx, 1973), and in toilet training (Foxx and Azrin, 1973). To date, however, the strategy remains untested in the schools, but one can think of numerous situations where it might be applied. For example, the strategy could be used with the student who carves on school desks, tears down a bulletin board, throws food in the cafeteria, litters the school grounds, or creates a mess in the classroom. In all of these instances, the student could be asked to put the environment in a better condition than existed before the misbehavior. The student who carves on a desk could be asked to sand that desk, plus one or more desks. The litterer could be asked to pick up more debris than he threw down.

Overcorrection offers several major advantages. First, the strategy has the potential for teaching desirable behavior by requiring the disruptive individual to improve the environment. He can then see the results of appropriate behavior. Other forms of punishment lack this benefit. Second, the strategy permits individuals to make amends for any damages they have caused. Overcorrection would permit them to set the situation straight. Overcorrection is unique in that people get a chance to improve the environment, and thus can begin to feel good about taking appropriate actions. Any bad relations between the disrupter and the educator should improve as the problem situation is overcorrected. Preliminary use of overcorrection also suggests that the strategy produces quick, permanent changes in behavior.

Harsh punishment is certainly uncalled for when one has the opportunity of using overcorrection.

Although overcorrection has considerable promise for reducing misbehaviors, use of the strategy could pose problems for the classroom teacher. Requiring a student to correct for more than damage done may be misunderstood by some administrators and parents. We would suggest that all parties concerned (parents, student, and administrators) be involved before the strategy is used. Also, teachers will need to withhold giving approval during overcorrection lest a student misbehave to receive praise for correcting the misdeed. As with all procedures—both positive and punitive—discretion is required if one is to be successful.

A Final Note of Caution

The forms of punishment described above may temporarily control certain disruptive behaviors, but in order to be effective, the techniques must be implemented properly. The checklist on pages 101-102 summarizes our guidelines for use of the punishment techniques described in this chapter.

Even if you follow every precaution in using punishment, you must realize that punishment per se is not a solution. Punishment teaches youngsters only what they should *not* do. It has never been an effective way of teaching what should be done. Positive strategies are needed to strengthen desired behaviors. At the most, punishment should serve only to suppress behaviors long enough for positive strategies to be implemented to strengthen desired responses. Even then, punishment is justified only in cases of repeated misconduct and for extreme misbehavior. Other uses of punishment would be insensitive to the well-being of both the user and the recipient. The individual who frequently uses punishment runs the risk of being reinforced for punishing others. If the punishment works, the user may become reluctant to explore other alternatives. Perhaps this is the greatest danger punishment holds for teachers. On the other hand, the recipient of nothing but punishment will become bewildered about what is correct behavior. That person may do little wrong, but will surely do little right. Being punished, but not rewarded, is a fate to which few of us aspire. We, therefore, caution that punishment be used infrequently. Remember, punishment can never be a substitute for all the positive things that constitute effective classroom management.

EVALUATION CHECKLIST FOR USE OF PUNISHMENT

Did you remember to:	Yes	No	Results and Recommendations

1. follow the general guidelines for using punishment by:
  A. clearly specifying the behaviors that will result in punishment?
  B. delivering punishment contingent on the specified behaviors?
  C. delivering the punishment immediately following the specified behavior?
  D. punishing each occurrence of the specified behavior?
  E. being consistent in punishing the same behaviors?			

2. use soft reprimands properly by:
  A. delivering reprimands only when you are able to move close to a student?
  B. avoiding berating the entire class?
  C. avoiding nagging?
  D. delivering infrequent disapproval?
  E. disapproving current behavior rather than behavior that occurred earlier?			

3. use time out appropriately by:
  A. determining whether classroom events are maintaining the inappropriate behavior?
  B. primarily limiting use of time out to younger students?
  C. providing a time out place devoid of opportunities for reinforcement?
  D. making sure the time out period is of short duration?
  E. remaining calm in taking students to the time out place?
  F. welcoming the student into the class after time out?			

EVALUATION CHECKLIST FOR USE OF PUNISHMENT (cont.)

Did you remember to:	Yes	No	Results and Recommendations
G. letting administrators and parents know of plans to use time out?			
4. use response cost properly by:			
A. limiting its use to highly disruptive students?			
B. making sure that what is withdrawn is not something that students are entitled to as a basic right?			
C. setting a reasonable price as the cost for inappropriate behavior?			
D. setting an upper limit on the number of times response cost will be imposed before more severe actions are taken?			
E. remaining calm while implementing the procedure?			
5. use overcorrection appropriately by:			
A. notifying administrators and parents prior to using this technique?			
B. determining whether the inappropriate behavior has resulted in damage that can be amended?			
C. determining what can be done to amend and improve the situation?			
D. withholding your attention during overcorrection so students will not misbehave to receive the attention during implementation of the technique?			

On Reasoning With Students

Some teachers contend that much classroom misbehavior can be controlled by reasoning with the student. If these teachers mean by reasoning with the students that students are involved in decision-making processes, then we agree. Many problems can be averted and others resolved by involving students in decisions about what is expected at school and what the consequences for different behaviors will be. The purpose for using any positive or punitive strategy should be aimed at helping students better their own behaviors. (We will provide details in Chapter Seven on how teachers can move students toward self-management.) But, if teachers mean by reasoning with students that the teachers will try to discover the reasons behind a student's behavior by delving into the student's past, then we disagree. This is not to say the past is unimportant. Students are influenced by their backgrounds. Knowledge of a student's home life or neighborhood experiences may give you ideas about what will work with a student. But too much emphasis on the past can be detrimental. Sometimes teachers will excuse repeated misconduct because of knowledge of a student's past history. They may comment, "With his background, he's lucky to be doing that well." Often students will learn they can use stories about their upbringing to "justify" misbehavior and to keep from learning new behavior.

What we are saying is that you could let reasoning or an attempt to understand students get out of hand. Teachers need not ask "Why did you do that?" for every disruptive act. Students may be unaware of why they behave as they do. Some students may give logical-sounding reasons that actually have minimal influence on their classroom behaviors. As we mentioned students behave appropriately because those behaviors are reinforced. They misbehave for the same reason. Our previous discussions should provide ways in which you can make desirable behaviors more reinforcing while minimizing the payoffs for undesirable behavior. By all means, involve your students. Let them help make choices regarding rewards and punishment for various behaviors. Use your knowledge of students in selecting appropriate activities. Just do not permit reasoning to keep you from helping students make needed changes.

Summary and Conclusion

Sometimes teachers are perplexed over the need to deal immediately with disruptive behaviors. They can think of few, if any, alternative ways of controlling misbehavior. Even when they do come up with an idea, too often it is to punish the misbehavior. This chapter has emphasized a number of positive strategies for managing disruptive classroom behaviors. Altering setting events, reinforcing incompatible behaviors, modeling, stimulus satiation, and extinction were discussed as possible alternatives to punishment. It is hoped that our review of these strategies will help you reduce the necessity for dealing punitively with students every time quick action is required. We recognized, of course, that no teacher ever has managed a class (and probably never can) without occasionally resorting to punishment. Hostile student acts that could result in personal injury and repeated misconduct often necessitate the use of punishment. So, rather than denying that punishment is used or pretending that teachers can rely solely on positive approaches, this chapter has focused on ways that punishment can be used more humanely and judiciously. Types of punishers were identified along with a discussion of the potential side effects of using harsh punishment. Guidelines for the effective use of punishment were also provided. Soft reprimands, time out, response cost, and overcorrection were suggested as mildly punitive strategies that seemed most acceptable for classroom use. Caution was advised even for using these forms of punishment lest you become dependent on temporary solutions rather than on seeking productive ways for teaching desired behaviors. The chapter concluded by stating that students can be involved in classroom decisions without dwelling on why they behave as they do.

After reading about all the alternatives for managing disruptive behaviors, you may be wondering "Which ones should I use?" Perhaps all of them. No strategy by itself is likely to be effective with every student. Your decision to select a particular approach may be governed by your own likes and dislikes, school policy, or parental responses. Or, you may have noticed that a student responds well to positive strategies. Perhaps you have even involved students in selecting consequences for inappropriate actions. It is unlikely that you would ever rely solely on one approach. You may make changes in setting events while using modeling and reinforcement of incompatible behaviors. You might also simultaneously be ignoring inappropriate acts. Further, you would never use punishment by itself. Once you have suppressed an undesirable response with punishment, you should certainly seize that opportunity to use positive means for teaching what you want. Your knowledge of alternatives merely increases the possibility that you can respond appropriately to student misbehavior. Certainly, you are better off being somewhat perplexed over having appropriate choices than wondering "Is there anything that can be done for this student?" Different strategies are at your disposal. Try them and make note of what works for you and your students.

Suggested Projects

1. Set aside a time for observing students in group work. Try identifying those students who provide assistance to others, who seem to get along well with everyone, and those who seem left out of activities. How might you rearrange setting events to facilitate greater productivity and involvement of all students?
2. Make a list of all the inappropriate behaviors that might occur in a classroom. For each behavior you have listed, identify an appropriate one you could reinforce that might be incompatible with the inappropriate.
3. List every appropriate behavior you occasionally call attention to and identify every possible student who might serve as a model. Did anyone get left out?
4. Describe a situation in which your own behavior was affected by the stimulus satiation. (Did you ever spend so much time with a friend that you tired of the relationship?) Next, describe a situation where stimulus satiation might help a student tire of an inappropriate behavior.
5. Think of a situation outside the classroom where you could employ extinction. What about ignoring an individual when he speaks negatively about others, while simultaneously reinforcing positive statements. Or, if you prefer a class project, think of a specific classroom behavior that you would like to extinguish.
6. Get others (perhaps students) to help you determine the potential punishers you are presently using. Do not overlook sarcasm, pointed fingers, frowns, and similar tactics. Describe the possible effects as well as the present effects of your actions.

7. Tape-record yourself delivering a reprimand to someone. Then, identify the ways in which your reprimand might be delivered more appropriately. Should certain words be omitted? Was the tone too harsh? What about the volume? Would another approach have been more advisable? Ask the other party for feedback about your reprimand.
8. Describe how a teacher might use time out on a playground.
9. Outline a token program that incorporates the principle of response cost.
10. How could you use overcorrection with a student who hits others?

REFERENCES

Ayllon, T. "Intensive treatment of psychotic behavior by stimulus satiation and food reinforcement." *Behavior Research and Therapy* 1 (1963): 53–61.

Ayllon, T., and Roberts, D. "Eliminating discipline problems by strengthening academic performance." *Journal of Applied Behavior Analysis* 7 (1974): 71–76.

Azrin, N. H.; Kaplan, S. J.; and Foxx, R. M. "Autism reversal: eliminating stereotyped self-stimulation of retarded individuals." *American Journal of Mental Deficiency* 78 (1973): 241–48.

Azrin, N. H.; Sneed, T. J.; and Foxx, R. M. "Dry bed: a rapid method of eliminating bedwetting (enuresis) of the retarded." *Behavior Research and Therapy* 11 (1973): 427-34.

Azrin, N. H., and Wesolowski, M. D. "Theft reversal: an overcorrection procedure for eliminating stealing by retarded persons." *Journal of Applied Behavior Analysis* 7 (1974): 577–81.

Becker, W. C.; Madsen, C. H.; Arnold, C. R.; and Thomas, D. R. "The contingent use of teacher attention and praising in reducing classroom behavior problems." *Journal of Special Education* 1 (1967): 287–307.

Broden, M.; Bruce, C.; Mitchell, M. A.; Carter, V.; and Hall, R. V. "Effects of teacher attention on attending behavior of two boys at adjacent desks." *Journal of Applied Behavior Analysis* 3 (1970): 199–203.

Brown, P., and Elliot, R. "Control of aggression in a nursery school class." *Journal of Experimental Child Psychology* 2 (1965): 102–07.

Foxx, R. M.; and Azrin, N. H. "Dry pants: a rapid method of toilet training children." *Behavior Research and Therapy* 11 (1973): 435–42

_____ ."Restitution: a method of eliminating aggressive-disruptive behavior of mentally retarded and brain-damaged patients." *Behavior Research and Therapy* 10 (1972): 15–27.

Hall, R. V.; Axelrod, S.; Foundoponlos, M.; Shellman, J.; Campbell, R. A.; and Cranston, S. S. "The effective use of punishment to modify behavior in the classroom." In K. D. and S. G. O'Leary (Eds.) *Classroom Management: The Successful Use of Behavior Modification.* New York: Pergamon Press, Inc., 1972.

Hall, R. V.; Fox, R.; Willard, D.; Goldsmith, L.; Emerson, M.; Owen, M.; Davis, F.; and Porcia, E. "The teacher as observer and experimenter in the modification of disputing and talking out behaviors." *Journal of Applied Behavior Analysis* 4 (1971): 141–49.

Kazdin, A. E. "The effect of vicarious reinforcement on attentive behavior in the classroom." *Journal of Applied Behavior Analysis* 6 (1973): 71-78.

LeBlanc, J. M.; Busby, H. H.; and Thomson, C. L. "The functions of time-out for changing the aggressive behaviors of a preschool child; a multiple-baseline analysis." In R. Ulrich, T. Stachnik, and J. Mabry (Eds.) *Control of Human Behavior: Behavior Modification in Education.* Glenview, Illinois: Scott, Foresman and Company, 1974.

Long, J. D., and Williams, R. L. "The comparative effectiveness of group and individually contingent free time with inner-city junior high school students." *Journal of Applied Behavior Analysis.* 6 (1973): 465–74.

Madsen, C. H.; Becker, W. C.; and Thomas, D. R. "Rules, praise, and ignoring: elements of elementary classroom control." *Journal of Applied Behavior Analysis* 1 (1968): 139–50.

Madsen, C. H., Jr.; Becker, W. C.; Thomas, D. R.; Koser, L.; and Plager, E. "An analysis of the reinforcing function of "sit down" commands." In R. K. Parker (Ed.) *Readings in Educational Psychology.* Boston: Allyn and Bacon, 1968.

The New York Times. "U.S. study finds violence rampant in nation's schools," March 19, 1976.

O'Leary, K. D. and Becker, W. C. "The effects of the intensity of a teacher's reprimands on children's behavior." *Journal of School Psychology* 7 (1968): 8–11

O'Leary, K. D.; Kaufman, K. F.; Kass, R.; and Drabman, R. "The effects of loud and soft reprimands on the behavior of disruptive students." *Exceptional Children* 37 (1970): 145–55.

Parker, R. D., and Walter, R. H. "Some factors influencing the efficacy of punishment training for inducing response inhibition." *Monographs of the Society for Research in Child Development,* 32(1) (1967).

Patterson, G. R. "An application of conditioning techniques to the control of a hyperactive child." In L. P. Ullmann and L. Krasner (Eds.) *Case Studies in Behavior Modification,* New York: Holt, Rinehart and Winston, 1965.

Solomon, R. L. "Punishment." *American Psychologist* 19 (1964): 239–53.

Solomon, R. W., and Wahler, R. G. "Peer reinforcement control of classroom problem behavior." *Journal of Applied Behavior Analysis* 6(1) (1973): 49–56.

Walters, R. H.; Parke, R.D.; and Cane, V. A. "Timing of punishment and the observation of consequences to others as determinants of response inhibition." *Journal of Experimental Child Psychology* 2 (1965): 10–30.

Zimmerman, E. H., and Zimmerman, J. "The alteration of behavior in a special classroom situation." *Journal of the Experimental Analysis of Behavior* 5 (1962): 59–60.

CHAPTER SIX

WORKING WITH OTHERS

The emphasis of this chapter is on identifying problem behaviors that may indicate a need for specialized services and on working with resource professionals in dealing with these special problems that may arise in the classroom.

Resource professionals commonly available in the schools include counselors, school psychologists, school nurses, speech pathologists, and school social workers. You may have already established a working relationship with many of these professionals. But knowing that some school systems employ few resource specialists, there is a discussion of community resources. In addition, suggestions for developing appropriate relationships with parents are provided.

Some Problems Require Referral

As a teacher, you have the primary responsibility for dealing with problems that may arise in your classroom. However, it is not expected that you can solve every problem for every child. Occasionally, students may have serious problems that will not change as a result of your efforts. Some of these problems may be related to poor health; others may be tied to poor home conditions and inadequate child care. Students with serious emotional problems and who cannot relate properly in the classroom may create management difficulties and may interfere with the learning of other students. At other times, normal students may engage in excessively disruptive behaviors that cannot be changed without careful planning. Success in teaching basic academic skills may well depend on whether problems such as these are remedied. Some students will require individual assistance from a specialist. Others can be dealt with in the classroom but may be more easily managed when resource consultation is obtained. Recognizing students who need specialized assistance and referring them to resource professionals should be considered part of a teacher's role.

Fortunately, teachers are realizing that being a "good" teacher does not mean that one must handle every problem alone. In fact, the idea that one is working alone can often result in loneliness and frustration. The feeling of support that can be gained from working with others and the opportunity to share ideas may very well be a major step in dealing with the problem. It is possible to be so closely involved with a situation that an objective assessment and plan cannot be made. In such cases, resource personnel may be able to provide the needed objectivity. The fact that a teacher asks for resource assistance should not be interpreted as a sign that he has failed. A team effort can pay big dividends in terms of effective classroom management.

Referrals In Perspective

Although every teacher may sometimes need to seek the assistance of resource personnel, a few teachers have mistaken expectations about referrals. They seek to use referrals as a way of giving their problems to someone else. Actually, few students who are referred to specialists are ever completely removed from the classroom. Resource people, such as counselors and school psychologists, often work with students in the setting (e.g., the classrooms) where the students are experiencing difficulty. Furthermore, most specialists will outline a major role for the teacher in helping the student. Those teachers who expect referrals to reduce their own responsibilities or to end in the removal of a student from their classes will undoubtedly be disappointed. This line of reasoning, of course, is unproductive. Rather than viewing referrals as a way of ridding yourself of problems, we hope you will see them as a way of sharpening your own skills through cooperative efforts with other professionals. Referrals work best when the people are working together to help students.

When To Refer

While teachers must avoid assuming that they can give their problems to others, teachers must remain willing to make needed referrals. A student *should* be referred to a resource specialist when he has a problem that the teacher cannot correct and that is interfering with academic achievement and personal development. And the teacher should never assume that someone else has already sought or will seek proper assistance. We know of one situation where a student wet himself daily at school for over six years before anyone tried to get the problem treated! Everybody took it for granted that the parents had done everything possible, but in fact, no assistance had been sought. Although this was probably a rare oversight, teachers in the higher grades often think that a problem has already been referred to someone at a lower level. If the student is still exhibiting signs of a serious problem, some teachers surmise that a specialist has been consulted and could do nothing for the student. When in doubt about whether a referral has been made or should be made, the teacher should always consult with resource professionals. The teacher and the resource person can then determine whether the student should be seen directly by the specialist.

Those problems that may require referral to a resource professional generally fall into seven categories: health related, visual, hearing, learning, behavior and emotional, speech, and home related. We will discuss each category and indicate specific behaviors that may alert the teachers to the possibility that referral to a resource specialist is advisable.

Health Related Problems

Health related problems represent an often unrecognized cause for poor academic achievement. Physical difficulties can impair students' performances regardless of their intellectual capacity. Health problems can also affect students' social behaviors. Very often, an irritable, inattentive or apathetic child is labeled immature or unmotivated, and the causes for his behavior are not investigated by the teacher or his parents. Students' health problems may occur in any classroom but are especially prevalent in school districts that serve a large proportion of students from low socioeconomic backgrounds. Behavior management techniques cannot successfully overcome problems related to poor student health.

Teachers should be aware of the more subtle behaviors that may be exhibited by students who have health related problems. Acute medical conditions (e.g., vomiting, diarrhea) are easily recognizable and usually result in immediate action by the teacher.

For example, the student may be sent to the school nurse or the parents may be notified to take the child home. Other symptoms are less easily recognizable as having a medical cause and may appear to be attention-getting behaviors. We have seen children who were originally labled as "behavior problems," but who were later diagnosed as having brain tumors or seizure disorders. Other health problems, such as inadequate nutrition, parasites, anemia, or lack of sleep, can affect a student's behavior in the classroom. Unless the cause of the problem is recognized, the behaviors may be interpreted as lack of motivation or lack of interest in learning. The latter problems are usually responsive to positive classroom management techniques. The former problems will need attention to the basic cause before the behaviors can be successfully changed.

Subtle signs that indicate that a student may need medical attention include:

1. Frequent complaints of headaches in the absence of other symptoms.
2. Lack of energy, appears to "drag," or is apathetic regarding classroom activities.
3. Often falls asleep in class.
4. Irritable or hyperactive behavior.
5. Frequent stumbling or falling.
6. Sudden episodes of staring during which there is no response to classroom events.
7. Frequent absences due to illness.
8. Suspected drug abuse.

Occasionally, you may encounter students who frequently complain of being sick. A teacher cannot always tell whether a child with physical complaints is malingering or whether the symptoms are, in fact, real. A medical examination can confirm or rule out whether medical treatment is needed. If the problem is found to be behavioral in nature, classroom management techniques may be successful in effecting change.

Visual Problems

Students with visual problems may not pay attention or may disrupt classroom activities when board work is being completed. Or they may have difficulty with close work and activities that require fine visual-motor coordination. Thus, they may fail to attempt these activities seriously. Some students may have poor visual acuity, that is, they cannot see either distant or near objects clearly. Other students may have normal visual acuity, but may not be able to see objects in proper perspective. You may notice that these students have difficulty with printing and drawing activities. For example, they reverse letters and rotate designs or they confuse letters that are similar (e.g., b and d, m and w). Students with these symptoms often have visual perceptual problems. Other symptoms that may alert teachers to a student's need for an eye examination include (Willgoose, 1969, p. 89):

1. Crossed, bloodshot, red, and swollen eyes. Pus and styes may be frequent.
2. Complaints of headaches, dizziness, eye pain, nausea, blurred or double vision, burning or itching lids. Some of these symptoms may also be present with serious medical disorders unrelated to eye problems.
3. Frequent stumbling or walking into objects. The student may not be able to estimate accurately the location of objects in space or may be unable to see those that are not in the direct line of vision.
4. Inability to distinguish colors. An occasional student may be colorblind.
5. Holding reading materials too close or too far away from the eyes. The student may close one eye or squint when looking at objects. Rubbing of eyes may be frequent.
6. Inability to see distant objects that can readily be seen by others. Some students may also have an undue sensitivity to light.

Vision screenings are sometimes routinely administered to all students by the school nurse or a public health nurse. An effort should be made to contact personally the parents of children whose screenings indicate the need for a more complete examination. It is not unusual for parents to postpone having the child's eyes checked because they lack the funds to pay for the examination. Teachers or school social workers can often assist the parents in locating resources that will help provide for the examination.

Hearing Problems

Teachers frequently encounter students who "tune out" or do not pay attention to class discussions. Usually the problem is behavioral in nature and is responsive to classroom management

techniques. However, an occasional cause of such behavior may be poor hearing acuity. The presence of two or more of the following symptoms suggests the need for a hearing evaluation:
1. Failure to pay attention in class.
2. Facial expression indicating lack of comprehension when oral directions are given.
3. Mispronunciation of words.
4. Mouth breathing.
5. Tendency to localize sound with one ear.
6. Unnatural voice pitch.
7. Complaints of earache; frequent ear rubbing.

Hearing screenings may be routinely completed by the school speech pathologist, the school nurse, or a public health nurse. As with abnormal vision screening, an effort should be made to contact personally the parents regarding the need for a more complete examination.

Learning Problems

Most teachers have no difficulty in recognizing students who do not learn as rapidly as others. Statements such as "Johnny just can't seem to catch on" or "Sue can't read even though she is in the fourth grade" are often made in response to students who fail to achieve at a level commensurate with their peers. Many of the students who fall behind academically exhibit undesirable behavior in school. They may fail to pay attention or may disrupt the class during learning activities. They may expend little effort in completing academic assignments. Some of these students may also be rejected by peers. When learning problems are present, working on social behaviors alone will be insufficient to insure that desired academic gains are made. It is possible to shape Johnny into a very obedient child, but he still may not know how to read or subtract.

Students with learning problems require a diagnostic workup to determine the major factors contributing to their poor academic performance. Some students may be found to have limited intellectual capacity. Others may have normal learning ability, but may not be achieving academically for other reasons. After the student has been evaluated, plans for remediation can be made. It is important to determine the level of functioning and the specific skills that have been mastered. Inappropriate social behaviors that occur as a result of a student's inability to achieve academically may improve when he is able to experience some success.

Behavior and Emotional Problems

Students who exhibit many inappropriate behaviors can easily tax a teacher's patience. As we discussed in Chapter Five, such children are often responding to environmental factors. For example, a student may be receiving peer or teacher attention for behaving inappropriately. These students usually respond well to the classroom management techniques described in earlier chapters. Sometimes, however, a student who engages in undesirable behavior may fail to respond to the classroom teacher. Consultative assistance should be requested when a teacher is unable to control the student's disruptive behavior. Students who exhibit sudden and persistent changes in learning or behavior patterns may require an evaluation prior to having a plan made for changing the behavior.

Sometimes a student may exhibit clearly inappropriate or even bizarre behaviors. Such a student requires individual assistance from a specialist. Presence of the following behaviors should alert the teacher to the need for a referral:

1. Appear to be "out of contact." The student may be zombie-like in appearance or he may be engrossed in a fantasy world.
2. Irrelevant or bizarre talk. A rare student may be echolalic. Or speech may be infantile.
3. Apparent aversion to people. The student may withdraw, isolate himself, and fail to communicate with others.
4. Self mutilation. For example, the student may continually pick and scratch at himself until be bleeds.
5. Continual rocking, finger wiggling, and extreme fascination with spinning objects.
6. Perseverative behavior, where the student exhibits the same behaviors over and over again.
7. Extremely aggressive or violent behavior.
8. Anti-social behavior, such as lying or stealing.
9. Inability to concentrate or to remain still for more than a few seconds at a time.
10. Excessively fearful or suspicious behavior.

Speech Problems

Students who are unable to pronounce words clearly or who stutter are sometimes mimicked and teased by their peers. Other students may have communication problems that are not as readily apparent but that interfere with their academic performance. For example, they may be unable to remember names of objects or to put events in a logical order. Referral to a specialist should be considered when the student exhibits the following difficulties in communicating (Zaslow, 1974):

1. Frequent misarticulation of words. The student may be difficult to understand.
2. Stuttering.
3. Abnormal voice quality. The child may have a very nasal or hoarse voice.
4. Inability to remember common words. The student may gesture and say "thing" or "stuff" in place of common words.
5. Tangential or irrelevant conversation.
6. Inability to follow oral directions.
7. Difficulty with tasks, such as sequencing problems or stories.
8. Frequent grammatical errors for age.
9. Difficulty in remembering what to say after raising hand in class. The student may appear to understand a process and then forget it or be unable to apply it to a different situation.

Home Related Problems

All children do not live in an adequate home environment. Many are deprived, both economically and emotionally. Some children are the victims of intentional neglect. In other cases, the parents may simply be unable to provide for their children. As a result, a student may be unkempt, improperly clothed, malnourished, and constantly sick. Lack of heat and irregular meals may be reported. Frequent absences from school are common. Children who are neglected or deprived are usually unable to perform at their potential level in school. Active intervention by a resource professional, such as a social worker, is often necessary in order to assist the family in obtaining needed resources and in improving the home environment.

In addition to living in a deprived environment, some children are the victims of child abuse. The incidence of child abuse is not restricted to lower socioeconomic families; middle and upper income parents also abuse their children. Shanas (1975) reports that the epidemic of child abuse is so widespread that all states in the union have either passed or updated laws requiring that child abuse or suspected abuse be reported. All teachers should become cognizant of the law and the reporting procedures of the state in which they are teaching. You can get this information by contacting your local social service agency, police department, and local or state government. Your principal will probably be aware of the law that applies in your state. It is our view that all suspected cases of child abuse should be reported whether or not it is mandated by law. Failure to do so may endanger the child's life, and will delay the time when the parents might be receiving needed professional assistance. In addition, what child can perform well in school or develop emotionally in a normal fashion when exposed to such conditions?

Making Referrals

Now that we have explored the kinds of problems that typically lead to referrals, let us briefly turn our attention to the procedures for making a referral to school resource people. Although each school system will have its own specific procedures, there are several general guidelines that should be followed. First, in requesting assistance from a school resource person, the teacher should be as precise as possible about the reason for the referral. Merely asking a resource person to "take a look at a student" leads to wasted time in which he tries to discover what the teacher already knows. Specific information about what the student is doing or is not doing should be provided. Otherwise, problems or real concern may be overlooked. The teacher may find it useful to keep a record of specific behaviors that the student exhibits to pass along to the resource person. We would also suggest that teachers avoid making broad complaints about the students. Statements about how a student is "wrecking the classroom" may be understandable in light of the problems teachers face, but such statements divert attention from the task of seeking solutions. Besides, restraint coupled with cooperative efforts to seek a solution should do a great deal to restore positive teacher attitudes toward students who are experiencing difficulties.

Second, after initial teacher contact with the school resource specialist, the parents should be involved if any special treatment is being comtemplated for the student. It is unnessary to contact a parent when a teacher is merely consulting with a resource person, but sound judgment dictates that parents be contacted before any special treatment, evaluation, or direct intervention by a specialist. Many school systems, in fact, require written permission from parents before a specialist evaluates a student. For example, when a student is referred to a school psychologist for evaluation, the parents should be given the following information: name and title of the person making the evaluation, the purpose of the evaluation, the date and time of the planned conference, and a description of their rights as parents to accept or reject the evaluation and any proposed educational plan. Written parental permission is also required in most school districts before making a change in a student's educational program. For instance, if it is recommended that a student spend part of the day in a resource room, the parents will probably need to give permission in writing. Even when such permission is not required, parents ought to be informed of the special problems others suggest their child is experiencing.

Although the resource specialist is often the person responsible for obtaining necessary permissions from parents, teachers should participate in parental conferences when special services are needed for a student. During the conference, the teacher can emphasize that the student is the major focus of concern. Occasionally, parents may state a feeling that the teacher would like to "get rid of the child" or that the teacher should know how to deal with the problem. It may be necessary to reiterate why a specialist should see the child and provide another professional opinion. Teachers can state a willingness to work with the resource specialist in following through on recommendations to indicate to the parents that they are not abandoning the student to others.

Directly related to the above procedures for making a referral is the often-asked question about where to refer certain types of problems. For example, teachers may notice that a student appears malnourished, has learning problems, and is frequenty absent from school. Should the teacher consult the school nurse, the school psychologist, or the school social worker? If possible, it would be appropriate to arrange a joint consultation with all of these professionals. If one is not feasible, referral to any of these professionals would be appropriate. One should not be unduly concerned about referring to the wrong person. In addition to being trained in their respective fields, resource professionals have also been taught to recognize problems that should be dealt with by other specialists. Most professionals are quick to admit the limits of their own competencies. When a student is found to have problems that require the attention of other professionals, the specialist who originally sees the student will arrange to have the appropriate specialist also see the student. If the resource person cannot arrange the proper consultation directly, the teacher will be notified as to the need for a different referral. Now let us take a close look at school resource personnel.

School Resource Specialists

Even though teachers are the primary source of referrals to resource personnel in the schools, many teachers and prospective teachers have never worked so closely with some of the specialists available in today's schools. Others are sometimes reluctant to make referrals because they have misconceptions about the duties performed by different specialists. Thus, much expertise available for assistance with students is never used. We are therefore providing you with information about the roles of school counselors, psychologists, speech pathologists, social workers, and nurses in dealing with students who have been referred for services. We also have a few suggestions about ways in which the teacher can coordinate with these professionals in providing optional help to students.

School Counselor

Originally, counselors were primarily assigned to secondary schools. Now many elementary schools, too, have them available. Counselors are trained to work with emotionally and socially maladjusted students. At other times, normal students who are engaged in decision-making may require counseling. At the secondary level, aptitude testing, educational placement, vocational guidance, and educational guidance may be part of their role. In addition, at both the elementary and secondary levels, counselors may provide consultative services regarding classroom management techniques.

Counselors often have heavy caseloads that prohibit them from working intensively with large numbers of students on an individual basis. Thus, group counseling sessions may be arranged for students who are experiencing similar problems. In addition to being more economical of the counselor's time, students who participate in group counseling can often help each other. At the elementary school level, counselors may work with entire classes by conducting class meetings. During these meetings, students have the opportunity to bring up problems of concern and to discuss them as a group. Or the counselor may propose a problem for discussion. Meetings are structured to minimize generalized complaining. One problem is usually dealt with at a time, and alternatives for solving the problem are suggested. When several consecutive meetings are held, students have the opportunity to try out proposed solutions and discuss the results in subsequent class meetings.

THE CASE OF THE DISAPPEARING ARTICLES

Mrs. Meadows, a fifth grade teacher, became concerned after several children reported that many of their personal articles, such as money or pencils, had disappeared. She had suspicions about who might be taking the articles, but no conclusive proof. After giving the matter some thought, she decided to consult the school counselor, Mr. Brown. He arranged to visit the classroom and conduct a series of class meetings in which the problem of the disappearing personal articles was raised. Students were encouraged to express how they perceived the situation and to propose solutions. One student suggested that perhaps the offending person did not realize how others felt when their personal things were taken. Another student suggested that the stolen goods be returned anonymously, with no questions asked and no accusations. The class agreed that this might be a good solution. A meeting was set for the following week in order to assess the effectiveness of the solution and to propose alternatives if needed.

Anandam and Williams (1971) propose a model for counseling services that differs from the traditional individual and group counseling model. They suggest that the counselor serve as a consultant to assist teachers in devising and carrying out behavior management plans in the classroom. The goal with this model is to change environmental conditions that may be affecting the student's behavior rather than attempting to change the student's behavior through traditional counseling. Counselors using this approach may observe in the classroom, assist in setting up a classroom management plan, monitor the effectiveness of the plan, and suggest modifications when necessary. The consultative approach can be especially productive when a teacher desires

"If you insist *on becoming a criminal, how about forgery or embezzling? You know — something nonviolent."*

assistance in dealing with problems of disruptive behavior. A joint effort between counselor and teacher is necessary, however, to insure success. Even though a teacher may be experiencing serious classroom management problems, most counselors would be hesitant to offer services unless the request is initiated by the teacher.

Individual and group counseling often work best when the referral is initiated by the student. Tesh (1974) suggests that teachers play a role in increasing the number of self-initiated referrals and in making the counselor more "visible" to the students by (1) providing opportunities for student-counselor contact by inviting the counselor into the classroom to present information, and by (2) making positive comments to students about the work of the counselor. Together, the teacher and counselor can become a strong team in maximizing all aspects of a student's development. Why don't you make an effort to get to know and use the counselor in your school? If you are still preparing to teach, you might ask one of your college professors to invite a counselor to be a guest speaker at an appropriate point in your studies.

School Psychologist

The school psychologist is one who has specialized in working with children and adolescents and who is trained to work in educational settings. Gilmore and Chandy (1973), in studying teachers' perceptions of school psychological services, rated the following groups as the most likely candidates for referrals to the school psychologist: children with apparent emotional problems, children who present behavior problems in the classroom, children who are intellectually retarded, and bright children who are low achievers. Fairchild (1974) analyzed the services performed by a school psychologist and found that school psychological services could be divided into four categories: assessment (testing and other activities related to diagnosis), intervention, evaluation of psychological services, and administration. In this study, a large proportion of the psychologist's time (39.7 percent) was found to be devoted to diagnostic activities. However, consultation was also found to consume a large share of time.

After receiving a referral, many school psychologists prefer to begin their services by observing the child in the classroom and on the playground. The observational period allows the psychologist to gain a picture of how the child functions in a natural setting. Through observation, environmental factors that may be influencing the child's behavior may also be detected. Many students are then scheduled for individual testing. The testing procedure allows the psychologist to sample the child's behavior under controlled conditions. Typically, assessment includes evaluation of intellectual functioning level, coordination skills, academic achievement, personality factors, and speech development. When indicated at the secondary level, interest and aptitude tests may also be administered. Students with learning problems may be given special tests designed to suggest channels through which learning may occur more easily. Test results and interpretations along with recommendations are usually provided in written form.

RETARDATION OR LEARNING DISABILITY?

By the time he reached seventh grade, Joe was seriously behind his peers in ability to read. As a result, he was experiencing difficulty in all academic areas and was falling farther and farther below grade level. Mrs. Green, his teacher, decided that Joe would be more appropriately placed in a special education class for the intellectually limited than in a regular seventh grade class where he could not keep up with other students. It was evident that his efforts were resulting in much frustration, and she felt that he was beginning to have emotional problems.

A referral to Mr. Blackwell, the school psychologist, was initiated and he arranged to see and evaluate Joe. The results of the evaluation indicated that his intellectual ability was normal. Mr. Blackwell arranged for more extensive evaluation to help determine the cause of Joe's learning disability and to assist in planning remedial learning activities. Joe was not appropriate for placement in a class for the intellectually limited. However, assistance from a learning resource teacher was arranged.

School psychologists generally confer with both parents and teachers regarding recommendations for students who have been referred for psychological services. They may also provide consultative assistance regarding implementation of the recommendations in the home or the classroom. When students who require the services of other professionals are identified, the psychologist usually arranges for referral to the appropriate specialist in the school or recommends a specialist in the community. The need for psychologists to be alert to problems other than the referring problem was well documented in Chrin (1974). Four cases were cited from his personal experience in which students with learning or behavior problems were subsequently found to have serious medical problems.

If teachers are to effectively utilize psychological services in the schools, they must be cognizant of the types of services the psychologist can render. School psychologists are usually willing to organize in-service training programs that focus on available services and on ways the services can be utilized. They may also conduct workshops on topics such as child management techniques or how to individualize instruction. Most school psychologists are interested in providing services that help prevent the occurrence of serious problems. The consultative approach, in which teachers are assisted in identifying and dealing with problems as they occur, appears to be a step in this direction.

The probability for successful intervention is increased if the intervention can be started before the child becomes unmanageable or fails completely.

School Nurse

Many school systems now employ school nurses. Students who display symptoms that suggest that they may have a health related problem are appropriate to refer for school health services. In general, the function of the school nurse may include the following activities (a joint statement of the American Nurses' Association and the American School Health Association, 1973):

1. Participation in obtaining a health history.
2. Performing a physical appraisal.
3. Evaluating developmental status.
4. Advising and counseling children, parents, and others.
5. Helping in the management of technologic, economic, and social influences affecting child health.
6. Participating in appropriate routine immunization programs.
7. Assessing and treating certain major illnesses and accidents of children.
8. Planning to meet the health needs of children in cooperation with physicians and other members of the health team.

Emphasis is now being placed on expanding the scope and training of the school nurse from the traditional model to that of the school nurse practitioner. The professional role of the nurse practitioner is significantly increased beyond that of the traditional school nurse and allows more responsibility in securing student health care in the schools. A study evaluating the impact of school nurse practitioners (Lewis, Lorimer, Lindeman, Palmer, and Lewis, 1974) found considerable enthusiasm by teachers and principals for increasing the scope and amount of nursing services available.

COPING WITH A MEDICAL PROBLEM

Mary Jane was a normal ninth grader who did well academically and generally got along well with other students in her classes. However, she was a victim of epilepsy, which could not be completely controlled by medication. As a result, she occasionally had a seizure that resulted in loss of consciousness. When this happened in class, other students became frightened. Following the seizures, they questioned her regarding what had happened. Mr. James, her homeroom teacher, referred Mary Jane to the school nurse, Mrs. Mason. Following the consultation, Mrs. Mason offered to talk with Mary Jane's classmates regarding seizure disorders, what happens during a seizure, and what should be done for someone who is having a seizure. Many students became very interested in the topic and were especially intrigued at the idea of electrical activity in the brain. The next time a seizure occurred in a classroom, they were able to react calmly and no longer treated Mary Jane with curiosity.

School nurses can make a constructive impact in helping solve classroom management problems only when students are referred for their services. In addition to handling minor illnesses and accidents, they may serve as consultants to parents, teachers, and administrators in identifying resources for community health care. When warranted, they may make home visits and consult with parents regarding the health of their child. Additional ways in which school nurses can assist teachers were suggested by Parker (1974):

1. Attending staffing conferences with other specialists and providing a diagnosis and plan for action on the referred child.
2. Assisting orthopedically or physically handicapped children by making special arrangements, such as transportation, seating, remedial physical education, adjustment of orthopedic devices, etc.
3. Making special arrangements for children with chronic impairments, such as diabetes or epilepsy, and providing teacher education regarding these conditions.
4. Serving as a resource teacher to educate pupils regarding impairments that classmates may have.
5. Serving as a resource teacher of health.
6. Serving as a health counselor and source of referral for diagnosis of VD and drug abuse.
7. Serving as a resource teacher in home and family living classes and in programs serving pregnant teenagers.

Speech Pathologist

It is not unusual for students with communication disorders to present classroom management problems by withdrawing or by becoming disruptive. The undesirable behaviors may, at times, represent an attempt to compensate for an inability to function satisfactorily in the classroom. Speech pathologists and speech therapists work with students who have communicative difficulties to assist them in overcoming these problems. These resource professionals are familiar to most teachers. You probably have one in your school.

IMPROVING ARTICULATION ABILITY

Louis was unable to pronounce the "R" and "L" sounds correctly. As a result, he said "wabbit" for "rabbit" and "wets" for "lets" Other students in the class began to minic his speech patterns and to refer to him as "Wouis." As a result, he gradually refused to participate in classroom discussions and to withdraw from interactions with other students in the class. From his behavior, he could be described as a very shy and unhappy child.

Mr. Johnson, his teacher, consulted with Mrs. Taylor, the pathologist, regarding Louis's speech problem and his behavior. Louis was scheduled for an evaluation and subsequent speech therapy. As his speech improved, he became more outgoing with other students and began to participate actively in class discussions.

Students with suspected problems in speech and language should be referred to the school speech patholgist (or therapist) for evaluation and remediation when indicated. In addition to working with students who cannot pronounce words plainly, speech specialists can assist teachers in dealing effectively with students who have limited hearing, who stutter, who have an abnormal voice quality, or who have delays in receptive or expressive language.

As with other referrals, the teacher should be specific when identifying suspected problems for a speech specialist. This information allows the screening or evaluation to be tailored to assess the suspected problem, and helps insure that some of the more subtle language difficulties are not overlooked.

Following the evaluation by a speech specialist, arrangements can be made for those students who require individual or group therapy. Any suggested remedial procedures are greatly enhanced when the teacher works with the speech specialist in stressing and reinforcing the development of the deficient language skills. For example, the speech pathologist may provide instructions for simple remedial exercises that can be used in the classroom, and may advise about other school activities for further assisting the child. Some communication disorders can be handled by the teacher through consultation with the speech pathologist. Severe problems usually require direct intervention by a specialist.

School Social Worker

Teachers expect to encounter few problems in working with middle and upper income parents. These parents are, for the most part, extremely interested in their children, and view education as a vehicle for "making it" in society. They tend to respond to requests for conferences and most of them attempt to do their part in working out problem situations. A few parents, however, do not respond to a teacher's notes or calls requesting consultation on their child. Lack of parental response is especially frequent in inner city and ghetto areas, but is not limited to these districts. Lack of parental involvement can be encountered in any school. A school social worker can be especially helpful in dealing with situations in which the parents make no voluntary contact with the schools.

HELPING PARENTS UNDERSTAND REASONS FOR A REFERRAL

Mrs. Greenlee was concerned because Linda was failing in class and appeared to have emotional problems. She decided that Linda should be seen by the school psychologist. As was school procedure, she sent home the standard permission form for Linda's parents to sign. The parents did not return the form, and refused to respond to any subsequent notes.

Mrs. Greenlee discussed the problem with Mrs. North, the school social worker, who arranged to visit Linda's parents in their home. At first the parents were hostile and repeatedly stated that their daughter "was not crazy." It became clear that the basic problem was the parents' lack of understanding regarding the purpose of the recommended psychological evaluation. The parents further assumed that only "crazy" people went to see psychologists. Mrs. North was able to explain the role of the school psychologist and to allay their fears that the teacher felt Linda was crazy. Mrs. North specifically stressed how the evaluation could be of benefit to Linda.

Following the visit of the social worker, Linda's parents signed a permission form to allow the testing to be completed. They also agreed to talk with the psychologist, teacher, and social worker following the evaluation in order to discuss findings and recommendations.

Many schools do not yet employ school social workers. However, the contribution these professionals can make to the development of school children is becoming increasingly recognized. During the past decades, social workers who were employed by school systems were usually assigned to the duty of dealing with truants, earning reputations as "truant officers" of sorts. The focus of school social work changed during the 1930s and 1940s to a casework model that deals with adjustment problems of children (Anderson, 1974). School social workers are the professionals in the schools who are most likely to work intensively with home and community related problems. Many social workers now serve as members of a school multidisciplinary team. This team usually includes the school psychologist, the speech pathologist, the school nurse, the counselor, the teacher, and perhaps the principal.

Specifically, what services can a school social worker offer to teachers? (1) Social workers are trained in home visitation and in assessment of family functioning. They can often provide information on students' home environments that is useful in explaining behaviors that occur in the classroom. For example, it may be found that some students do not have a stable home environment. One or both of the parents may be alcoholic, and the child may be shifted from relative to relative. These children may fail to learn and may appear apathetic or withdrawn, or perhaps they may be aggressive toward other students. The social worker can perform an important function in establishing rapport with the family and in assisting them in obtaining needed aid to help provide adequately for the physical and emotional needs of their children.

(2) A social worker can help the teacher by communicating positive aspects of the child's experience to the family. Through getting to know and working with the family, he may be able to improve communication between the teacher and parents. (3) Due to training emphasis on working with families and communities, a school social worker can usually offer expertise in dealing with problems of truancy. (4) Social workers can work with other school professionals and students to change conditions in the school that may serve as contributing factors to students' problems (Nieberl, 1974). Students who are interested in exploring and making changes in school procedures may receive a helping hand from the school social worker.

Teachers should attempt to maintain regular communication and should not be expected to fill this role. However, when communication problems are encountered, the social worker may be able to serve as a liaison between home and school in effecting the needed changes.

Community Resources For The Child

Unfortunately, some schools employ only a limited number of resource persons, or special services may not be readily available due to the large number of students who must be served by a limited number of professionals. What alternatives are open to the teacher with students who require more assistance than can be provided in the classroom? In such situations, community resources will need to be explored to determine whether the needed assistance can be provided outside the school.

Identify Community Resources

Large metropolitan areas usually have the most specialized resource services available. Smaller towns may be more limited, but usually provide medical and mental health services. Universities may offer multidisciplinary diagnostic teams. When school resources are limited, it is worthwhile to spend the time necessary to determine what services are available in the community. It may be helpful to set up a card file to include relevant information, such as the name of the resource, the types of services offered, fees charged, eligibility criteria for clients, the referral procedure, and the name of the contact person for the resource. Many agencies publish brochures that are helpful in outlining services offered. Often the school system itself will maintain a list of available services and make the list available to teachers.

Schedule a Parent Conference

Once a problem has been identified, the next step in securing resource assistance for a student, when services are unavailable through the school system, is to arrange a parent conference. The child's problem should be explained to the parents, and their interpretation of it should be considered. In particular, the recommendation for referral should be discussed and specific reasons why additional services are felt to be needed should be provided. Conti (1973), in investigating follow-up referrals recommended by school psychologists, found that 76 percent of the families referred for counseling made contact with counseling services, and that 85 percent of the families referred for other services (medical, educational, psychiatric, special school placement) made at least an initial contact.

During the parent conference, the teachers may need to reassure the parents of the need for outside services and to explain why the school is currently unable to offer the services. The teacher should also indicate what kind of cooperative efforts will exist among the school, the teacher, and the community agency. Also, if the teacher wishes to be informed of the results of any studies, parents should be asked to sign a release form giving permission for the information to be sent to the school. Otherwise, confidentiality laws will prohibit the teacher and school system from receiving copies of diagnostic workups or progress reports. It is the parents' right, of course, to refuse release of the information.

Arrange for Referral to a Community Resource

Agencies differ in their referral procedures. Some will accept referrals only from professionals. Others require that the initial contact be made by the family. In cases where a medical problem is suspected, the teacher should advise the parents to consult their physician, or to take the child to a local health department or clinic. If the child's problem is felt to be emotional, parents may be advised to call the local mental health center, or to consult a private psychologist or psychiatrist. Children with multiple problems may benefit from intensive diagnosis through a multidisciplinary evaluation unit that combines medical, psychological, speech, and social service assessments. Some units also provide specialized studies such as chromosomal analysis and genetic counseling to the family when indicated. Diagnostic teams associated with a university often provide the most thorough professional teamwork.

Children with suspected hearing defects or communication disorders may benefit from referral to a speech and hearing clinic. Frequently, such clinics are associated with universities, but private clinics may also be available. Public health departments usually screen hearing and vision and may provide needed medical attention for families who cannot afford private services. Departments of public welfare offer financial assistance as well as social services to eligible clients and may be a resource agency that can be utilized by some families. Vocational rehabilitation centers offer counseling and training to handicapped individuals.

Community Resources Of The Teacher

The emphasis in this chapter has been on locating and arranging for resource assistance to students who require special services. Sometimes teachers also desire consultative assistance in designing and implementing classroom management plans, or in developing programs for use in the classroom. Perhaps the teacher lacks expertise in dealing with a problem that can be handled in the classroom, and would appreciate consultative help regarding remedial activities. What are some possible resources that the teacher can explore when consultative assistance and classroom aid is desired? Our suggestions may provide a starting point in identifying available resources.

Multidisciplinary Evaluation and/or Treatment Units

Professionals associated with multidisciplinary teams may offer consultative services to teachers regarding management of their patients. These teams usually include physicians, psychologists, speech pathologists, social workers, nutritionists, and nurses. A comprehensive team evaluation usually includes input from each of these professionals. If a student has been referred for evaluation or treatment, it may be helpful to request professional consultation in order to follow through with recommendations in the classroom. The probability of success in working with any problem is maximized when individuals who deal with the problem are aware of the goals and are consistent in the way they deal with the problem.

Departments of Speech and Hearing or Special Education

Given the current emphasis on mainstreaming the handicapped, some teachers may be faced with students who demand specialized expertise not possessed by the teacher. For example, a student with a severe hearing impairment may be able to communicate with others only through the use of sign language, or a student with cerebral palsy may receive part of his instruction in the regular classroom. In such cases, it may be possible to arrange for consultative services through a speech and hearing department or a special education department associated with a university or college. Sometimes college students can be placed as student teachers or on practicum assignments, thereby providing assistance in a specialized area. Students who are majoring in the education of the deaf or physically handicapped could teach the needed skills to the teacher and students while receiving credit from their university.

Schools of Social Work
Social work students are required to spend a designated amount of time in field practice during their training. Teachers may be able to get a student placed in their school. If home or community related problems are interfering with effective classroom management, social work assistance may be especially helpful.

Departments of Psychology and Education
Most departments of psychology and education are seeking field experiences for their students. Some professors may be willing to supervise projects in which graduate students assist the teacher in developing, implementing, and monitoring a classroom management program. Other college professors may seek opportunities for research and may be willing to commit time to working with a teacher in exchange for the opportunity to develop a program that will implement a research idea. Thus, practical assistance may be made available to a teacher who lacks the basic knowledge to develop a program. When adequate supervision can be arranged, graduate students may also be able to provide counseling and evaluation services.

Work Through The Proper Channels

Several simple procedures should be followed when arranging to use a resource person from the community. (1) The teacher may wish to talk with colleagues to determine whether they are interested in utilizing resource consultation. (2) The teacher should confer with the school principal, explain the problem, outline the types of assistance sought, and obtain permission and support for inviting outside personnel into the classroom. Sometimes the principal must check with his supervisor before giving final permission. The teacher should not invite visitors into the classroom until official permission has been received and only then may the university or community agency be contacted to arrange for professional or student consultation.

Teachers who elect to use free consultative services from local colleges or universities should give consideration to factors that could pose potential problems. (1) Cooperation with a research project may be a prerequisite for receiving the consultative help. In many cases, the goals of the research mesh with those of the teacher and no problems are encountered. However, some projects may entail restrictions and procedures that may be unacceptable. The obligations of each party should be clearly spelled out before any work is done.

(2) Using the classroom for research purposes, while providing much worthwhile data for education, usually involves using students as research subjects. Most researchers abide by ethical standards when conducting research. However, teachers and principals who cooperate with research projects should be familiar with *Ethical Principles in the Conduct of Research with Human Participants* (1973), provided by the American Psychological Association.

(3) College students may lack the experience and expertise to provide answers to many of the problems encountered in the classroom. Undergraduates can usually do creditable jobs as classroom observers, tutors, and special unit or project instructors, but usually lack the training and experience to assist teachers in developing sophisticated classroom management programs. However, graduate students, especially those who are training at the doctoral level, may be able to provide very helpful consultative assistance.

Develop A Relationship With Parents

Both parents and teachers would like to have students become happy, productive citizens. Parental support and cooperation are important factors in reaching this goal. Fortunately, most parents are willing to help in whatever way they can to insure that their child gets a good education. Unfortunately, they are often not consulted unless their child has broken a rule, failed to attend school regularly, or is not keeping pace academically. Few teachers remember that parents would also like to know when their child has performed especially well or has exhibited behaviors of which they can be proud. All students exhibit some desirable behavior, even though rates of progress may be different. Students who are chronic disruptive influences occasionally sit quietly. Parents appreciate knowing when a child has had a good day. They like to know when their child is making progress, even though it may be minimal. Parents can be expected to be more cooperative with the teacher and the school when they receive positive, as well as negative, feedback about their child.

We are not saying that all desirable behaviors exhibited by students can be communicated to parents. Few teachers have time to write even monthly notes. However, seeing that each child carries home a note once each grading period commending him for some appropriate behavior can do much to increase positive attitudes of parents and improve teacher-parent relationships.

Parents usually know their children well. They know their children's likes and dislikes and can often tell a teacher what works and does not work with them. They can frequently provide information that is helpful in reducing inappropriate classroom behaviors or in increasing desired behaviors. Occasionally, students present problems that are more easily resolved through a joint effort than through either the parents or the teacher working alone.

TALKING DURING CLASS ACTIVITIES

Jimmy, an excellent student academically, often disobeyed Mrs. Sims's rule about talking to other students during class periods. Continued admonitions to pay attention and stop talking seemed to have little effect. As a last resort, Mrs. Sims contacted Jimmy's parents and asked them to come to school for a parent conference. The problems with Jimmy were carefully explained and her genuine interest in him was communicated. At this point, she admitted that she was unable to solve the problem of his talking during class activities.

Jimmy's parents, in exploring the situation with Mrs. Sims, discovered that he was invariably seated near Timmy, a neighbor and close friend. The suggestion was made that Jimmy's chair be moved in order not to be near Timmy during academic lessons. Mrs. Sims was hesitant about following this suggestion because it violated her policy of allowing students the freedom to choose their own seats and class partners for study.

Further discussion revealed that Jimmy often completed his work before many of the other students, thus providing unscheduled free time. His parents offered to send reading materials to keep him occupied during this time. This solution was helpful in reducing the chattering problem but did not eliminate the disruptive behavior completely. As a last resort, the parents' suggestion of moving Jimmy away from his friend was followed, and resulted in elimination of his disruptive behavior. Having the parents help make the decision eliminated the possibility that misunderstanding might occur when Jimmy was no longer allowed to choose his own chair.

It is the authors' opinion that parent-teacher conferences should be scheduled at least twice each year. Some schools have experimented with the idea of providing student holidays during which time parents are scheduled for private conferences with the teacher. This approach appears to be working as long as flexibility is included for those parents who cannot manage a conference during regular school hours. Scheduling a few conferences in the evenings to accommodate parents who work during the day is usually sufficient.

Teachers occasionally feel overwhelmed and perhaps frightened at the idea of conducting individual parent conferences. Parents may feel the same way about meeting and talking with teachers. They may be especially concerned lest they be told that their child is not doing as well as they thought or hoped. Thus, both the teacher and parent may be ill at ease at the initial meeting. Beginning the conference on a positive note can help to ease tensions. Showing the parents examples of their child's work that are especially commendable or that demonstrate progress is a good way to begin. Relating a positive behavioral incident involving their child can also increase positive parent responses and thus help reduce teacher tensions. Behavior and academic areas that need improvement should be discussed. However, we suggest that the conference begin and end on a *positive* note.

Sometimes teachers are faced with parents who are dissatisfied with something that has happened in class or with some school procedure. Parents can occasionally be irate. How does a teacher deal with an angry parent in order to dissipate some of the emotional aspects of the encounter and reap benefits for the child from the interaction? How does a teacher refrain from also becoming angry in such a situation? The following suggestions may be helpful in coping with such a crisis. (1) Refuse to conduct the conference in the classroom with students present or outside the door of the classroom during school hours. Firmly insist on setting up a conference for a later hour. (2) In conducting the conference, attempt to remain unemotional. Try not to take comments personally. Remember, the parents are probably concerned and upset over what they *perceive* is happening to their child. And their perception may or may not be correct. Try to determine how the parents perceive the incident in question and solicit their views regarding a solution. Expect that the views will often be expressed though unsolicited! (3) Responding to parental feelings behind the statements (c.g., "You are really concerned about..." or "... makes you very angry."), rather than the content, can communicate to parents that one really understands and reduces the likelihood of direct conflict. (4) Help the parents explore the ramifications of different solutions with the goal of providing for the best interests of the child. Attempt to work out at least a beginning solution to the problem. If possible, arrange for both the parents and the teacher to be responsible for some aspect of implementation. (5) Arrange for continued communication. Ask the parents to call and report, positively or negatively, on what has happened since the conference. And do not be afraid to say "I don't know," "I have tried," "I need your advice," "This may not work," "I may be wrong," or "Call me if things don't go well." Hearing teachers admit that they may not always be right can go a long way in defusing an irate parent.

In summary, when should a teacher contact a parent? (1) On a regular basis to report progress of the child. An effort should be made to report positive as well as negative events. (2) When management problems that are not easily remedied are occurring with their child. An honest discussion of the problem and proposed solutions should be provided, and parent input should be considered. (3) When a new or novel behavior management program is planned for the classroom. Parents should be informed regarding the rationale and goals, and any questions should be dealt with in an honest and forthright manner. It is important to avoid becoming defensive regarding plans. (4) When a child requires referral for an evaluation or a change in his educational placement is planned.

Summary

The focus of this chapter has been on working with resource professionals to maximize the development of children with problems that cannot be adequately handled by the classroom teacher. It was pointed out that teachers should become cognizant of the types of specialized services available in the schools and should refer students with special problems for assistance. Indicators for referral were provided for health related, hearing, visual, learning, behavior, emotional, speech, and home related problems. The types of services provided by counselors, school psychologists, speech pathologists, school nurses, and school social workers were discussed.

Consideration was given to working with community agencies and private professionals when specialists are unavailable in the school. The procedure for making referrals was delineated. The importance of working with parents was stressed, and suggestions for improving relationships between teachers and parents were provided. Possibilities for consultative assistance to the teacher through community sources were also considered.

Resource specialists can contribute a great deal to the development of students who require their services. Alertness in detecting serious problems is important. However, it should be stressed that few children in a classroom need specialized assistance beyond what the teacher can provide. Every child who misbehaves is not an appropriate referral for a specialist. The techniques described in Chapters Three and Five remain appropriate for dealing with most of the problems that you will encounter in daily teaching.

Suggested Projects

1. Enlist the aid of colleagues in surveying community resources. Consider inviting representatives of agencies to a faculty meeting, in-service training program, or to a college class to provide information on services provided by the agency and to answer questions.
2. Suggest that a faculty meeting, in-service program, or college class be devoted to ways of working effectively with other professional partners in the schools.
3. Develop a procedure for staffing children with special problems. Who would you include on the team? How would you provide for follow-up and changes in recommendations when needed?
4. Devise a plan to insure that all the parents receive positive communication about some aspect of their children's behavior at least once every grading period. Try to send these notes at times other than the grading period.

5. Consider the following cases. How would you deal with each one?
   a. A fifteen-year-old girl recently had a baby. She wishes to continue her education, but does not fit in well at school. How would you assist her in coping with her problem and in completing high school?
   b. A 10-year-old boy continually falls asleep in class. Repeated admonitions by his teacher appear to have no effect on his behavior. What course of action would you suggest for this child?
   c. A thirteen-year-old girl has always been a cooperative student. Academically, she does average work. During a period of a few weeks, a change is observed in her behavior. She begins to fall down academically, disrupt class, and fail to cooperate with many requests.
   d. A seven-year-old child refuses to come to school. His parents are at a loss as to how to cope with his behavior. As his teacher, you are concerned. His parents also call you asking for help in dealing with the child.
   e. A nine-year-old boy begins to stutter when called on in class. Stuttering seems to be worse when he is under pressure. Although you do not wish to precipitate the stuttering episodes, you feel that class participation is important.
6. Practice writing anecdotal records that describe student behaviors in specific terms. That is, what does he do, or not do, that is a problem? What specifically does he do that is indicative of progress? Be sure to avoid value judgments. You can do this by sticking with observable behaviors.

REFERENCES

Anandam, K., and Williams, R. L., "A model for consultation with classroom teachers on behavior management." *The School Counselor* 18 (1971): 253–59.

Anderson, R. "School social work: The promise of a team model." *Child Welfare* 53 (1974): 524–30.

Chrin, M. J. "The school psychologist." *Today's Education* 63 (1974): 23–24.

Conti, A. P. "A follow-up investigation of families referred to outside agencies." *Journal of School Psychology* 11 (1973): 215–23.

Ethical principles in the conduct of research with human participants. Washington, D.C.: American Psychological Association, 1973.

Fairchild, T. N. "An analysis of the services performed by a school psychologist in an urban area: implications for training programs." *Psychology in the Schools* 11 (1974): 274–81.

Gilmore, G. E., and Chandy, J. "Teachers' perceptions of school psychological services." *Journal of School Psychology* 11 (1963): 139–47.

Lewis, C. E.; Lorimer, A.; Lindeman, C.; Palmer, B. B.; and Lewis, M. A. "An evaluation of the impact of school nurse practioners." *The Journal of School Health* 44 (1974): 331–35.

Nieberl, H. R. "The school social worker." *Today's Education* 63 (1974): 25–26.

Parker, N. "The school nurse." *Today's Education* 63 (1974): 30–31.

"Recommendations on educational preparation and definition of the expanded role and functions of the school nurse practioner." American Nurses' Association and American School Health Association, *Journal of School Health* 43 (1973): 594–97.

Shanas, B. "Child abuse: A killer teachers can help control." *Phi Delta Kappan* 56 (1975): 479–82.

Tesh, B. D. "The counselor." *Today's Education* 63 (1974): 20–22.

Willgoose, C. E. *Health education in the elementary school*. Philadelphia: W. B. Saunders Company, 1969.

Zaslow, E. L. "The speech pathologist." *Today's Education* 63 (1974): 27–29.

CHAPTER SEVEN

GUIDING STUDENTS TOWARD SELF-MANAGEMENT

All of the preceding chapters have emphasized things *teachers* can do to manage students. While there is considerable merit in the teacher's knowing how to manage student behaviors, a number of important reasons exist for teaching students how to manage themselves effectively. First, teachers may actually have a broader, more significant influence by teaching students to govern themselves. If teachers indefinitely assume responsibility for student actions, students may become overly dependent on them. They may behave appropriately only when the teacher is present to offer reinforcement or punishment. Absence of the teacher could produce frustration and inappropriate private behavior. Second, students may perform better both socially and academically when given opportunities to manage themselves. Many students express resentment over having all decisions made by others. One frequently hears the complaint, "They [adults] want us to grow up, but won't let us." Third, students are often the only ones in a position to know what changes are needed. Teachers can never hope to know all the inner thoughts of students, nor can they expect to see everything that happens in and out of the classroom. Fourth, and closely related to the previous point, students may know better than the teacher what is reinforcing and punishing. Desired changes are possible only when meaningful consequences are applied for designated behavior. Finally, many of the ethical and legal problems concerning the use of various rewards and punishers can be avoided when students are involved in decision-making processes. Too often, teachers get themselves into difficulty by making all decisions regarding the behavior of others.

Many benefits are obviously associated with the development of self-management skills. Of course, self-management never completely frees a student of all dependence on others. Support, encouragement, and feedback from teachers and other significant persons will always be needed. An ultimate goal of education has always been to help youngsters achieve enough independence to live happy, productive lives. This chapter is aimed at just that goal by emphasizing ways in which self-management can be attained, and focuses specifically on the origins of self-management, techniques for achieving self-management, and major concerns related to self-management.

Origins of Self-Management

In order for teachers to help youngsters become more self-directive, they must have a clear conception of how individuals develop self-management skills. Some teachers have the idea that self-control or self-management (we will use the terms interchangeably) is a matter of personal desire. They contend that if students really "want to," they can overcome bad habits and develop new skills. Teachers with this belief often exhort students to "set your mind to it," "show a little initiative," and "come in here with a better attitude." All responsibility for change is thus attributed to some internal reservoir of strength. Students who fail to change may be regarded as lacking "what it takes." Certainly, no one would deny that desire is an indispensable ingredient in self-management, but desire alone is hardly a sufficient condition for the development of self-control. Students must also know *how* to produce wanted changes (Williams and Long, 1975).[1] Desire by itself in no way provides the knowledge that is essential for developing new behaviors.

Even when desire is recognized as an essential part of self-management, the question of where desire comes from still remains. Does it come solely from within the person, or is it influenced by environmental factors? We believe the latter gives students the impetus to want to improve. Social contacts at school, encouragement from the teacher, success experiences, a setting

---

[1] For a more comprehensive discussion of the philosophical foundations of self-management as well as specific details for developing self-management in various social and academic areas, see R. L. Williams and J. D. Long, *Toward A Self-Managed Life Style* (Boston: Houghton Mifflin, 1975).

conducive to self-improvement, and a host of other environmental events can influence how much desire a student displays. Students who receive reinforcement for their efforts in self-management are undoubtedly going to exhibit more interest in it than students who are mostly overlooked and punished for their failures. The kind of feedback that students receive can also influence what students "want" to do. Highly specific feedback, for example, can convey necessary information about how a person can change, whereas global feedback may only discourage by leaving too much doubt about how change can be accomplished. Similarly, the example set by the teacher can influence the amount of desire shown by students. Teachers who are self-confident will probably imbue others with confidence in themselves. Our point is this: teachers can create desire. There is no longer any reason to assume that students either do or do not have it.

Just as teachers can help increase students' desires to improve, they can also help students develop the knowledge required to produce wanted changes. Students do not come into the world knowing how to study more effectively, improve interpersonal relationships, or break a distasteful habit. They must learn to manage these areas of their lives in much the same way that they learn any academic skill. Of course, students sometimes accidentally discover how to manage a specific behavior without the help of others. But such changes are of minimal benefit when the individual cannot deliberately sustain desired changes. Even when students can sustain a behavioral change in one area, they may be unable to manage other dimensions of their lives. Effective self-management exists only when students learn to produce deliberate, long-lasting outcomes in whatever areas they choose. And, we believe that effective self-management can be best achieved when students are taught specific self-management strategies. By teaching them, the teacher can avoid the frustrations and chaos that could result from assuming that students know how to control themselves if only given the chance. With that in mind, let us take a look at a few of the strategies that can help students gain better control over their own behaviors.

Techniques of Self-Management

The techniques discussed in earlier chapters clearly represent ways that teachers can manage student behaviors. Yet, many of the same techniques can be used by students to change their own behaviors. Indeed, there are many that can be used in achieving self-control. In this section, we will discuss the most frequently used techniques of self-management: self-recording, control of setting events, managing consequences, self-verbalization, and behaviorial contracting. Although we will discuss each technique separately, they apparently can be used in combination. Most students will probably benefit by learning all the strategies, and can then select what seems most natural and effective to themselves.

Self-Recording

Students are often unaware of how they actually behave. Some of their behavior may occur so automatically that it completely escapes their attention. Other behavior by itself may seem too unimportant to notice. However, by recording their own actions, students can become more aware of how they appear to others. That feedback alone may be all that is required to produce a change in behavior.

BILL LEARNS SOMETHING ABOUT HIMSELF

Bill was a seventh grader who seemed to be constantly complaining. He complained about his classmates, his assignments, the weather, the school. You name it and Bill had a complaint. Mrs. Vandiford, his teacher, was worried about the effect his complaining was having on his relationships with others. Finally, Mrs. Vandiford asked him if he knew how he appeared to others. Bill remarked that he seldom complained and was generally regarded as a likeable person. Mrs. Vandiford then asked him if he would be willing to keep a record of the times he expressed dissatisfaction to others. Together, Bill and Mrs. Vandiford made a list of his frequent complaints. He was to check any of the items that he complained about during the day and discuss these with Mrs. Vandiford each day at the close of school.

Something remarkable happened when Bill began self-recording. His behavior improved immediately. Maybe he was trying to avoid complaining to prove something to Mrs. Vandiford or perhaps he was learning something about himself that he did not like. In any event, Bill was a changed person. Mrs. Vandiford felt so differently about him that she began praising him more for his cooperative behaviors. Within three weeks he asked to discontinue self-recording, but he continued to complain less throughout the term.

While the results obtained in the preceding illustration may be more dramatic than can normally be expected, research does support the assumption that self-recording can result in greater self-control. For example, Broden, Hall, and Mitts (1971) found that self-recording was effective in increasing attention to classroom lesson activities of an eighth grade girl. In a second experiment, Broden and her colleagues found that self-recording also reduced talking out without permission by an eighth grade boy, but in this case self-recording eventually lost much of its effectiveness. The researchers suggested that external support might be needed to sustain the behavior changes initiated through self-recording. They commented that "perhaps the most promising feature of self-recording will be to use it as a procedure for initiating desirable levels of appropriate behavior to a point where the teacher can more easily reinforce the desired behavior with attention, praise, grades, or other reinforcers available in the classroom." Of course, when desirable behavior changes become habitual, self-recording and reinforcement could be gradually reduced.

Other researchers have also found self-recording to be useful in improving self-control. Long and Williams (1976), for instance, employed self-recording with a group of retarded adolescents in a special education class. They had each student maintain a point sheet on which he recorded points for appropriate responses. The students logged points for being ready to start lessons, having appropriate materials, completing assignments, working quietly for specified time periods, and similar activities. Recording of points increased levels of appropriate responding for the group by approximately 10 percent during spelling and by approximately 15 percent during reading. Similarly, Johnson and White (1971) found that self-recording of study behavior improved the course grades of a group of college students. Self-recording could presumably be used with any group of students and for any behavior.

Although self-recording may prove beneficial for many students, several research studies (Bolstad and Johnson, 1972; Long and Williams, 1976; Mahoney, Moura, and Wade, 1973) reveal that it can be more effective when combined with other techniques. Teachers can use self-recording with external reinforcements they provide, with other self-management techniques, or with both. We will discuss a number of possible combinations in the remainder of the chapter. Teachers should also recognize that self-recording is not foolproof. It may work best for those students who seek help and who are already highly motivated to change. Some students may also be inaccurate about the data they report. The accuracy of reports can probably be improved by the teacher's taking time to compare occasionally student records with those of the teacher. Because many students may also be unfamiliar with the alternative methods of self-recording, let us turn briefly to a discussion of those methods.

Methods of recording. The methods selected for record keeping will depend largely upon the behaviors themselves. Behaviors that have a discrete beginning and end lend themselves to a *frequency count.* This involves nothing more than counting the number of times the behavior occurs. Number of positive and negative comments, questions asked or answered, times late for class, and similar behaviors can be subjected to a frequency count assessment. Paper and pencil or a mechanical counter (e.g., a golf counter) can be used by students in making frequency counts. Some behaviors that occur over extended time periods do not readily lend themselves to the frequency count. Time spent studying, working on special projects, sleeping, being off the task, and other continuing kinds of behavior can best be subjected to a *time assessment.* The simplest way to measure this type of behavior is with a stopwatch. Sometimes rather than making a continuous frequency count or an assessment of all the time spent at a specific behavior, a student could be assisted in *sampling* a behavior at designated intervals. Sampling can provide valuable information if a behavior occurs frequently enough so that periodic measures are representative of the student's total behavior pattern.

Students will probably want to devise their own record keeping systems. However, a form similar to Table 7–1 could be used for recording most classroom behaviors. Students need only to (1) make tally marks in the appropriate block every time the behavior in question occurs or to (2) record the amount of time spent on the task. Although separate tables would be required for each behavior, students generally would be recording only one or two behaviors. Expending effort trying to record a host of different behaviors could be counterproductive anyway. It is better to begin by gaining control over one behavior than by having grandiose plans to change everything simultaneously.

Irrespective of the method used for recording behaviors, students will probably find it helpful to graph their behavior on a daily basis. Sometimes a student feels that no progress is being made. Graphing will permit students to make a quick assessment of themselves. Even seeing that slight improvements are occur-

TABLE 7-1
BEHAVIOR RECORD SHEET

TIME or CLASS	M	T	W	Th	F	M	T	W	Th	F
8:00– 8:55 Math										
9:00– 9:55 English										
10:00– 10:55 History										
11:00– 11:55 Study Hall										
12:00– 12:55 Lunch										
1:00– 1:55 French										
2:00– 2:55 Science										
TOTALS										

BEHAVIOR _____

ring can be extremely helpful in maintaining self-management efforts. Everyone likes to know that progress is being made.

A form similar to Figure 7–1 could be used for graphing specified behavors. In constructing such a graph, the ordinate (vertical line) can be used to indicate the frequency of a given behavior or the amount of time spent on a behavior, and the abscissa (horizontal line), to indicate the days. The student will need only to plot the level (frequency, or amount of time) of the behavior on the appropriate day. Drawing a line connecting the plots on the various days will yield a picture of the behavior.

In establishing a record-keeping system, students should consider measuring not only their behavior but also the events that precede and follow behavior. Recording the events that occur before and after a behavior may provide clues as to why the behavior occurs and what needs to be done to change it. For example, behavior is often associated with particular times of the day, persons, and setting. A student whose friends support him after every misdeed may want to ask that their reinforcement be directed at other behaviors. Students who fail to take into account the events that make them angry, happy, critical, cooperative, and so on, possess only limited potential for producing worthwhile changes in themselves.

Control of Setting Events

An effective self-management technique alluded to in the previous section as well as in Chapters Two and Five is the control of

FIGURE 7–1
DAILY BEHAVIOR GRAPH

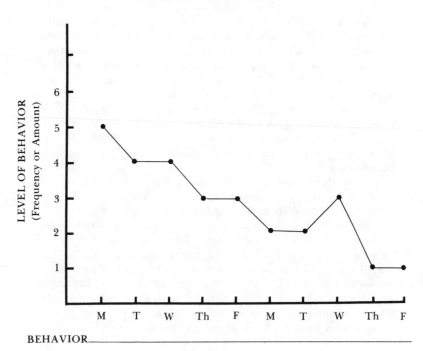

setting events. Many students, however, have never consciously considered how setting events influence their behaviors. Thus, teachers will have to encourage students to think about the factors that influence people to behave as they do. Teachers may find it helpful to ask students the amount of time taken on a task, the order in which activities are undertaken, how other people, places, the composition of a group, and other environmental stimuli effect their behavior. Students will usually recognize immediately that their behavior does not occur in a vacuum. The most important point for them to learn, though, is not *why* they behave as they do, but, rather, that something can be done to change their behavior.

MANAGING STUDY BEHAVIOR

Joe, a tenth grader at Central High School, was taking his first course in French. He had never been one to study much because most things seemed to come easy for him. French was different. Joe was falling farther behind each day. He tried to make himself study, but usually got little accomplished. Joe really wanted to do better so he asked his teacher, Mr. Pharr, for help. Together they discussed Joe's behavior. Joe explained that frequently he tried studying in the school library, but that he generally wound up talking with other students or looking at girls. Mr. Pharr and Joe figured that for Joe the library was a stimulus for socializing, not study. Joe also indicated that he sometimes tried studying in the afternoon immediately after school, but this was ordinarily a time when he played tag football or just goofed off with his friends. Because the afternoon hours were associated with other acts, Mr. Pharr and Joe reasoned that time was also triggering nonstudy behaviors.

To remedy the situation, Mr. Pharr and Joe devised a plan that would help Joe control setting events. He set aside one hour after dinner for study. Although he decided to begin by studying fifteen minutes each day and gradually build up to the full hour, no other activity was planned during the study hour. He thought a gradual process would be better than expecting a radical change. Joe also decided to set aside a portion of his room for study, and cleared his personal desk of all pictures, magazines, and materials that might generate thinking about anything other than school work. Mr. Pharr and Joe agreed that controlling setting events at least was a step towards greater self-management of study.

Generally, controlling setting events involves either (1) reducing the stimuli that trigger unwanted behavior, or (2) increasing the stimuli that foster desired behaviors. Students who refuse to bring nonacademic materials to class (unless requested to do so) would be reducing the range of stimuli that could generate unwanted behavior. Similarly, students who elect not to sit beside friends who encourage inappropriate talking, who limit the distractions occurring during their study time, or who avoid associating with peers who insist on misbehaving are reducing the probability of misbehaving themselves. Since students cannot always avoid troublesome situations, they may have to concentrate on increasing the stimuli that foster desired behaviors. Strengthening desired behavior, of course, will also invariably reduce unwanted behavior. Shy students who associate with persons who encourage socializing increase the probability of overcoming their shyness. Likewise, students who bring appropriate texts and materials to class and those who develop a schedule for their daily activities increase the stimuli that can cue appropriate behavior. With the teacher's help, they can probably think of numerous other stimuli that can be altered to better control their own behavior.

Managing Consequences

Although self-recording and control of setting events alone may produce changes in behavior, these techniques are often most helpful when combined with the management of behavioral consequences. It is the events that occur after an individual has emitted a behavior that largely determine whether the behavior will occur again. So, to maintain desired changes that result from self-recording, control of setting events, or other techniques, teachers should consider helping students manage the consequences of their own behavior. In fact, several studies have found self-management of reinforcers to be superior to teacher management of reinforcers. Lovitt and Curtiss (1969), for example, found that the academic response rate of a twelve-year-old student was higher when the student specified the requirements for reinforcement than when only the teacher specified the requirements. Similarly, Bolstad and Johnson (1972) revealed that self-regulation of reinforcers (self-recording and self-dispensing of reinforcers) was more effective in reducing disruptiveness among the most disruptive students in ten first and second grade classrooms than was teacher regulation of reinforcers. Other studies (Ballard and Glynn, 1975; Glynn, 1970; Long and Williams, 1976) attest to the potential usefulness of self-rewards. More studies (e.g., Arwood, Williams, and Long, 1974; Dickinson, 1968; Williams, Long, and Yoakley, 1973) also suggest that students' input into the management of punishers can improve their behaviors.

Teachers who are interested in having students manage behavioral consequences need to consider a number of factors related to the effective control of consequences. (1) Since accurate management of reinforcers and punishers necessitates record keeping, students may need assistance in developing adequate record keeping systems. The previous discussion on self-recording should be helpful in this respect. (2) Research (Kanfer and Duerfeldt, 1967) suggests that individuals reinforce themselves in much the same way as they have been reinforced by others. Thus, teachers may find that they can increase student success with self-reinforcement by first successfully reinforcing desired student behaviors. Teachers who find that students are either too lenient or too stringent with rewards and punishers may want to consider how they are responding to the students. (3) Students may need assistance in identifying appropriate reinforcers and punishers. Atkins and Williams (1972) found that students often have difficulty identifying stimuli that actually serve as reinforcers. Perhaps this is a result of limited exposure to a variety of potential reinforcers. In any event, students must realize that something is reinforcing only if it will maintain or strengthen behavior for them. Teachers may find that having the entire class make a list of potential reinforcers will increase the likelihood that each student identifies appropriate reinforcers. Likewise, students may require assistance in identifying potential punishers. Many students probably think that punishment must be either a paddling, a trip to the principal's office, or suspension. They may never have considered the possibility of withholding a privilege, overcorrection, or other type 2 punisher. (4) If students are to manage behavior consequences, they should receive instructions on how to use rewards and punishers effectively. The same principles that were discussed in earlier chapters regarding teachers' use of rewards and punishers should apply when students themselves control the consequences. For instance, applying reinforcers contingent on desired behavior, applying them immediately, and using a variety of reinforcers are just as applicable when self-applied as when externally controlled. Students can achieve success with self-management of consequences only to the extent that they know how to control those consequences properly.

KAY MAKES A DECISION

Kay was a ninth grade general math student who spent a lot of time reading paperbacks when she was supposed to be working math problems. Kay frequently got into trouble with her math teacher, Mr. Carson, because of her reading. Mr. Carson did not really mind if Kay spent some time reading as long as she paid attention to explanations and completed the assignments. One day, during a conversation with Kay, Mr. Carson suggested that she try doing math first and afterwards rewarding herself with reading. Mr. Carson explained that his suggestion was based on the Premack principle, which asserts that a highly probable activity (e.g., reading) could be used to reinforce a less probable activity (e.g., math). Kay simply would need to do the less probable activity first. Since Mr. Carson was primarily interested in Kay's completing her assignments, he suggested that she monitor her own behavior and reward herself whenever she completed the daily assignments. Kay felt Mr. Carson was being very fair so she decided to follow his suggestion.

Self-Verbalization

Most persons from time to time vocally or subvocally instruct themselves on what they should and should not do in given situations. Athletes, for example, often tell themselves "watch the ball," "wait for the signal before starting," "keep your head down." Similarly, some motorists, when caught in a line of traffic, remind themselves to "be patient," "remain calm," or "try to be courteous to other drivers." There are also occasions in the classroom when self-verbalization could help students achieve better self-control. They can verbalize to themselves to control their anger, reduce anxiety associated with giving a speech, and be more positive in the comments they make to others. Unfortunately, some students, especially those who are impulsive, have probably never learned self-verbalization as a means of gaining greater self-control. Such students act before they think. As with other self-management techniques, however, students can learn to self-verbalize.

An interesting study by Meichenbaum and Goodman (1971) demonstrated that a group of second graders who were exhibiting hyperactive and impulsive behaviors could be trained to talk to themselves as a means of developing self-control. They were trained on a variety of tasks, such as copying line patterns and coloring figures within boundaries. During the training sessions, students individually observed the experimenter perform the task while giving himself instructions out loud. The following is an example of the experimenter's self-verbalizations:

> Okay, what is it I have to do? You want me to copy the picture with the different lines. I have to go slow and be careful. Okay, draw the lines down, down, good; then to the right, that's it; now down some more and to the left. Good, I'm doing fine so far. Remember, go slow. Now back up again. No, I was supposed to go down. That's okay. Just erase the line carefully . . . . Good. Even if I make an error I can go on slowly and carefully. Okay, I have to go down now. Finished. I did it. (117)

After observing the experimenter, each student performed the task while instructing himself aloud. Next, he performed the task while whispering instructions. Finally, he performed the task covertly (without lip movements). The idea was to help him internalize self-instructions. The students who received training in self-verbalization subsequently performed significantly better on psychometric tests which measured cognitive impulsivity, performance I.Q., and motor ability than did control students who were exposed to the training tasks, but were not trained to self-verbalize.

O'Leary (1969) has also demonstrated the utility of teaching students to self-verbalize. In his experiment, first grade boys received a marble for pressing a telegraph key. The marbles could be exchanged for prizes; the more marbles a boy earned, the more valuable a prize he could purchase. But the boys were supposed to press the key only when a certain stimulus was flashed on a screen. Eventually the boys were left alone to perform the task while the experimenter observed through a one-way mirror. Boys who were trained to verbalize aloud what they could and could not do were less likely to "cheat" on the experimental task than boys who were simply told what was right and wrong. You can probably think of similar situations in a classroom when students might be trained to verbalize rules out loud. Having students tell themselves what they have done correctly on academic and social tasks might also cue further appropriate behavior. In the following illustration, at least one student used self-verbalization to control his temper.

TOM HAS A TEMPER

Tom was a sixth grader who had never learned to control his temper. If someone said something that Tom did not like, he generally wanted to fight. Sometimes he cursed and threw things when he got mad. Everybody seemed afraid to say anything to him. Tom's problem reached a critical level one day when he cursed the teacher. The teacher sent for the principal, and Tom was threatened with expulsion unless he could learn to control his temper. He was later given an opportunity to talk with the school counselor. They discussed the possibility of self-verbalization. The counselor suggested that Tom start subvocalizing what could happen to him if he continued to lose his temper. Tom made a list of the things he could tell himself. Thoughts like "You could hurt someone or get hurt," "How must you look to others," "How would you feel if someone reacted that way towards you" and "Try saying something nice and see how . . . will respond" were included on Tom's list. He even thought about counting to ten when he got mad before he would make any response. The counselor had Tom visualize different problem situations and verbalize what he would say to himself when those situations arose.

Behaviorial Contracting

Behavioral contracting is a technique that appears to have wide use with students of vastly different backgrounds. Researchers have found contracting to be effective in improving classroom behaviors of inner-city blacks (Sapp, 1971), disadvantaged white students (Arwood, Williams, and Long, 1974), and economically advantaged students (Williams, Long, and Yoakley, 1973). Others have found contracts to be useful with students adjudged to be potential school dropouts (Homme, 1966) and in treating problems ranging from hyperaggressivity and stealing to under-achievement and school phobia (Cantrell, Cantrell, Huddleston, and Woolridge, 1969). In all of these studies, school personnel got more of what they wanted (e.g., improved academic and social behaviors from students) by reaching agreements with students on how they could earn existing reinforcers (e.g., free time, grades).

The real value of contracting, however, does not lie in its potential to alter problem behaviors. Other techniques can also produce worthwhile changes. Perhaps its greatest value is that it provides a means by which students can progress from external control of their lives by others towards greater degrees of self-management. Contracting enables teachers and students to work out *mutual agreements* in which students can assume more control as they demonstrate greater personal responsibility. Thus, teachers are not confronted with surrendering total responsibility for self-control to students without knowing first how they will respond.

One of the most practical plans for using contracting to help students achieve greater self-control has been developed by Homme, Csanyi, Gonzales, and Rechs (1970). Their plan involves five stages. The first is labeled manager-controlled contracting. In this stage, an adult manager (e.g., a teacher) determines the task to be performed and the amount of reinforcement to be given for completion of the task. Upon acceptance of the contract by the child and completion of the assigned task, the manager delivers the reinforcer. In the second stage the child may be given joint control of the task or of the reinforcer. If this is done, the manager maintains complete control of the reinforcer. If the child jointly controls the reinforcer, the manager determines the task. You will notice that at this stage greater control is still maintained by the adult manager. The third stage, however, involves equal control by the manager and the child. In this stage, the child can (1) jointly control both the task and the amount of reinforcement, (2) completely control the task, while the manager controls the amount of reinforcement, or (3) the amount of reinforcement, while the manager controls the task. The fourth stage shifts even more control to the child. The child can take complete control of the task while jointly sharing control over the reinforcer, or he can take complete control over the reinforcer while sharing control of the task. The fifth and final stage is labeled child-controlled contracting. In this one, the child has control over both the task and the reinforcer. Homme and his colleagues suggest that students achieve success with each stage and with each possible type of control before advancing to the next stage. We think their plan has considerable merit because it allows a gradual transition to self-control as students demonstrate ability to assume new responsibilities. Of course, you and your students must be the ultimate judges of whether you want to use contracts and, if so, how those contracts will be managed.

At this point, you realize that both teachers and students can exercise varying amounts of control in contracting, but you may still be wondering about some of the mechanics of implementing a contract, whether it should be positive or negative, whether it should be used with individuals or groups, or how to go about obtaining student participation. While contracting can consist of agreements to do or not to do certain things, we believe that it should emphasize primarily positive behaviors. This does not mean that rewards should never be withdrawn for engaging in inappropriate acts. However, contracts that clearly identify appropriate behaviors and the payoffs for engaging in those behaviors should be far more acceptable to teachers and students than those that emphasize mainly negative behaviors. Also, the contracting process can be greatly simplified by remembering that the same principles of reinforcement discussed in Chapter Four and mentioned in this chapter under the topic of managing behavioral consequences should be followed, no matter who con-

"This is Wally. He's representing us in our homework negotiations."

trols the contract. As to whether contracts should be used with individuals or with groups, our own experiences suggest that they can be effective regardless of whether they are used with individuals, small groups, or large classes. You will probably find that using the same format for an entire class is less demanding on you than developing unique instruments for each student. Of course, the tasks that students perform and the reinforcers they select can vary without having different contracts. Students can simply be given a choice of different rewards once they have completed their assigned task. Finally, regarding the involvement of students, we have found a straightforward approach to be best. We ask them for their opinions about what they consider to be appropriate and inappropriate classroom behaviors and what the consequences (rewards and punishers) should be for those behaviors. Students can also be involved in the wording of written contracts, in maintaining records, in providing feedback about how well contracting is working, and in making recommendations for new ways of using contracts. Students at all ages will have ideas to share if their teacher is willing to solicit and reinforce student input. Possibly the most important consideration in implementing a contract is the teacher's willingness to involve students. After all, contracting connotes cooperation.

Although you and your students could devise many different types of contracts, you are probably interested in seeing at least one illustration of a contract. Below is a behavioral contract negotiated between an eighth grade teacher and her students. Perhaps you and your students would be interested in trying a similar contract in your class.

CONTRACT FOR CLASSWORK

I agree to abide by the following conditions and consequences during Math 101. I understand this agreement will be renegotiated after a trial period of three weeks or before that time if a majority of students or the teacher feels another agreement would be more desirable.

Conditions
(1) To be seated and ready to begin work before the tardy bell rings.
(2) To bring pencil, paper, and appropriate books to class.
(3) To avoid engaging in loud talking, noise making, and other behaviors that could interfere with others' learning.
(4) To complete class assignments each day and correct all errors on previous day's assignments.

Consequences
Free time will be available for approximately ten minutes at the end of each class period for those who have met all the preceding conditions for that day. During free time, eligible persons may read comics, draw, listen to radio (if earplugs are used), play math games provided, work on other assignments, or engage in other relaxing activities that do not distrub others. Those who do not meet the conditions or those who disturb others during free time must begin their homework assignment or proceed with other assigned tasks.

Signed: _____
          (Student)

_____
(Teacher)

Concerns About Self-Management

As with most other strategies, the proposed use of self-management raises a number of important concerns for teachers. One is whether self-management techniques are really suitable to some students. Teachers ask, "Aren't elementary students a little too young for self-management?" "Can *this* work with retarded students?" "Don't some students have to be directed by others?" These are legitimate questions for which absolute answers are difficult, if not impossible, to give. However, we believe that most students are capable of far more self-control than they presently exert. Even nursery school children can be given opportunities at self-management. While this may involve only giving the child a choice between, say, two activities, making choices is a step towards greater self-management. Retarded students, too, are probably more capable of demonstrating personal responsibility than many persons think. Of course, some students may require more direction than others. But self-control itself presumably begins with someone else providing proper control of the environment. Students who have been exposed to a setting in which others have failed to recognize and reward desired changes may initially need a great deal of direction. Once they receive consistent, predictable responses from important people, they can also move to higher levels of self-management. Certainly, you will agree that students can develop self-management skills only when people in authority provide the opportunities for learning those skills.

Another concern of teachers is the trustworthiness of students who are given chances to govern themselves. Teachers tell us that a few students cannot be trusted to make accurate self-reports; other students reportedly give themselves reinforcers they have not earned. Admittedly, the accuracy of self-reports may vary from student to student. Some students may be lenient in rewarding themselves. However, "cheating" can be reduced through teacher surveillance. Students can also be "caught" keeping inaccurate records and improperly reinforcing themselves. Remember, those behaviors that get rewarded by the teacher will undoubtedly increase in frequency.

The long-range effects of self-management are also a matter of concern. Teachers rightfully wonder if students who enthusiastically undertake self-management will continue with those efforts. Perseverance with self-management efforts is probably affected both by the goal an individual sets and the motivation to reach that goal. Teachers can help with both. They can caution students against setting unrealistic goals that are apt to create frustration and failure. Teachers can also praise students as they progress toward their goals. Few things are more motivating than positive responses from significant adults. Initial enthusiasm can be sustained, but teacher support may be required for some time. No one is suggesting that students can be turned loose and expected to perform indefinitely without any assistance.

Occasionally, teachers also express concern over the amount of teacher involvement that is required with teaching self-management. Any teacher who has ever involved students in classroom management knows that a great deal of teacher time and effort *is* required. We do not deny it. No worthwhile procedure can be implemented without expending some energy. And although self-management tactics may initially require a lot from the teacher, we think a savings will result in the long run. Teachers who are eventually freed from continuous monitoring and reinforcement of every student's behavior, for example, can devote more time to those who demand more individual assistance. In addition, students who learn to assess their own behaviors, set appropriate tasks for themselves, and provide their own rewards are on the way to becoming responsible citizens. And that is what the business of education is all about.

Summary

In this chapter, we have pointed out that the ultimate goal of all education is for students to be able to manage their own behaviors. We have suggested that students do not learn self-responsibility by having others continuously manage their affairs or by having total control thrust upon them. Instead, the chapter stressed that students learn self-management in the same way any other task is learned. It was posited that teachers must help students become aware of alternative ways for achieving self-control, as well as provide opportunities for students to use those techniques. Self-recording, control of setting events, management of rewards and punishers, self-verbalization, and contracting were discussed as the principal techniques of self-control. A number of important concerns that teachers raise about self-control were also discussed. While the chapter has revealed the broad potential of self-management, teachers surely recognize that self-management does not free one from dependence on others. Concern, encouragement, and positive responses from others will always be needed. But coupled with external support, the learning of self-management skills is of unlimited value.

Suggested Projects

1. Develop a form that students could use for recording the amount of time they spend studying. How about a form for recording appropriate classroom behaviors, such as being on time, having paper and pencil, completing class assignments, and so on?
2. Identify all the potential setting events that a student might need to control in order to reduce talking out in class, or to improve the quality of work completed.
3. Have a group of students make a list of potential rewards that could be used in connection with classroom self-management projects.
4. Describe the self-verbalization that a student might emit to reduce anxiety associated with giving a speech or taking an exam.
5. Develop a contract among parents, child, and teacher to govern the completion of homework assignments.

REFERENCES

Arwood, B.; Williams, R. L.; and Long, J. D. "The effects of behavior contracts and behavior proclamations on social conduct and academic achievement in a ninth grade English class." *Adolescence* 9 (1974): 425–36.

Atkins, J. W., and Williams, R. L. "The utility of self-report in determining reinforcement priorities of primary school children." *Journal of Educational Research* 65 (1972): 324–28.

Ballard, K. D., and Glynn, T. "Behavioral self-management in story writing with elementary school children." *Journal of Applied Behavior Analysis* 8 (1975): 387–98.

Bolstad, O. D., and Johnson, S. M. "Self-regulation in the modification of disruptive classroom behavior." *Journal of Applied Behavior Analysis* 4 (1972): 443–54.

Broden, M.; Hall, R. V.; and Mitts, B. "The effect of self-recording on the classroom behavior of two eighth-grade students." *Journal of Applied Behavior Analysis* 4 (1971): 191–99.

Cantrell, R. P.; Cantrell, M. L.; Huddleston, C. M.; and Woolridge, R. L. "Contingency contracting with school problems." *Journal of Applied Behavior Analysis* 2 (1969): 215–20.

Dickinson, D. J., "Changing behavioral techniques," *Journal of School Psychology* 6 (1968): 278-83.

Glynn, E. L. "Changing applications of self-determined reinforcement." *Journal of Applied Behavior Analysis* 3 (1970): 123–32.

Homme, L. "Human motivation and the environment." In N. Haring and R. Whelan (Eds.) *The learning environment: relationship to be-*

havior modification and implications for special education. Lawrence: University Press of Kansas, 1966.

Homme, L.; Csanyi, A. P.; Gonzales, M. A.; and Rechs, J. R. *How to use contingency contracting in the classroom.* Champaign, Illinois: Research Press, 1970.

Johnson, S. M., and White, G. "Self-observation as an agent of behavioral change." *Behavior Therapy* 2 (1971): 488–97.

Kanfer, F. H., and Duerfeldt, P. H. "Motivational properties of self-reinforcement," *Perceptual and Motor Skills* 25 (1967): 237–46.

Long, J. D., and Williams, R. L. "The utility of self-management procedures in modifying the classroom behaviors of mentally retarded adolescents." *Adolescence* 41 (1976): 29–38.

Lovitt, T. C., and Curtiss, K. A. "Academic response rate as a function of teacher- and self-imposed contingencies." *Journal of Applied Behavior Analysis* 2 (1969): 49–53.

Mahoney, M. J.; Moura, N. G. M.; and Wade, T. C. "The relative efficacy of self-reward, self-punishment, and self-monitoring techniques for weight loss." *Journal of Consulting and Clinical Psychology* 40 (1973): 404–7.

Michenbaum, D. H., and Goodman, J. "Training impulsive children to talk to themselves: A means of developing self-control." *Journal of Abnormal Psychology* 77 (1971): 115–26.

O'Leary, K. D. "The effects of self-instruction on immoral behavior." *Journal of Experimental Child Psychology* 6 (1968): 297-301.

Sapp, G. L. "The application of contingency management systems to the classroom behavior of Negro adolescents." Paper presented at the meeting of the American Personnel and Guidance Association, Atlantic City, April, 1971.

Williams, R. L., and Long, J.D. *Toward a self-managed life style.* Boston: Houghton Mifflin, 1975.

Williams, R. L.; Long, J. D.; and Yoakley, R. W. "The utility of behavior contracts and behavior proclamations with advantaged senior high school students." *Journal of School Psychology* 10 (1972): 329–38.

CHAPTER EIGHT

RIGHT AND WRONG: ETHICAL AND LEGAL PROBLEMS OF CLASSROOM MANAGEMENT

The classroom management strategies described in the previous chapters share a common purpose: behavior change. In most classrooms, techniques such as these are used to change students' behavior to conform to a teacher's concept of desirable or appropriate behavior. Many decisions pertaining to classroom management rest entirely on a teacher's sense of right and wrong. Ethical and legal questions may thus arise concerning the goals of behavior change and the techniques that are used to reach these goals. Teachers are unlikely to use methods that are regarded as immoral, and rightly so. Similarly, few teachers use techniques that are clearly in violation of the law. Unfortunately, decisions must sometimes be made in haste and may be based on misconceptions regarding the appropriateness of various behavior change techniques. Often the laws pertaining to school affairs are learned after a costly mistake has been made.

In this chapter, we will examine some of the ethical and legal aspects of classroom control. Each teacher must make a personal decision regarding the behaviors to be changed in the classroom and the techniques that will be used to change these behaviors. Critical study of the issues can facilitate the decision-making process, and may clarify previous misconceptions regarding various classroom management techniques. Careful deliberation of the issues should assist you in making your own decisions in the classroom.

Ethical Issues: Goals of Behavior Change

The accepted goal of the educational process is to change behavior. Six year olds entering first grade have few academic skills, and their social behaviors are immature. At the end of their public school training, however, society expects that they have advanced academic skills and are able to function in a mature and independent fashion. The entire schooling process, then, from grades one through twelve is directed toward this goal.

In recent years, new techniques have been developed that increase the probability that desired behavior changes will occur. Thus, questions pertaining to the goals of behavior change have become more crucial. Several issues have been raised and are debated in the professional literature. For example, are behavior management techniques being used merely to induce conformity? Who should make the decisions regarding which behaviors should be changed? Does one stifle creativity when students are required to conform to the expectations of the teacher?

In addition to issues pertaining to the goals of behavior change, questions have been raised concerning behavior change methodology. Is it ethical to use extrinsic or tangible rewards? When rewards are made contingent on desired behavior, is the process equal to bribery? Does a reward system teach undesirable values: for example, that desired aims can be bought? What are the long-range effects of providing tangible rewards? Other issues revolve around the use of negative behavior control techniques. Is it ethical to use criticism or corporal punishment to control students' behavior? What are the problems in using response cost or time out? Should aversive methods be used in the classroom? These questions and others may arise in any consideration of classroom control. The decision you make regarding these issues will be reflected in the goals you set in the classroom and the methods you use to reach them.

Purpose of Behavior Change

Traditionally teachers have been considered successful when they are able to maintain a classroom in which students sit quietly, refrain from talking to their neighbors, and raise their hands for permission to speak. The emphasis in recent years on informal education and open classrooms has changed this situation for some teachers. However, many principals still expect to see a quiet, well-controlled group of students when they patrol the halls or walk into a classroom.

In reviewing behavior-management studies that appeared in the *Journal of Applied Behavior Analysis* from 1968 to 1970, Winett and Winkler (1972) concluded that children in these studies were not allowed to be children, but, rather, were required to be docile, quiet, and obedient "young adults." Suggesting that such a situation might be destructive, these authors proposed that a freer classroom atmosphere can also be conducive to learning. Further, they contended that behavior modification techniques are often used to maintain the status quo in the schools.

Certainly, the question of whether behavior change techniques should be used to induce conformity of this type must be taken seriously. We would agree with most educators that academic skills cannot be taught successfully when the classroom climate is utter chaos. There appears to be a need to maintain a classroom environment that enables students to hear class discussions and to finish assigned seatwork without constant interruption. On the other hand, maintaining a quiet classroom sometimes becomes the primary goal. Students' mastery of academic and independent thinking skills becomes secondary to their demeanor in the classroom. Sophistication in the area of behavior control techniques has increased the probability that teachers will attain whatever goals are set in the classroom. Consequently, the goals of behavior change become critically important.

Personal Versus Institutional Goals.   McIntire (1974) contends that many schools propose to provide students with the requisite skills necessary for attainment of personal goals that will increase happiness and effectiveness. However, schools may have a number of other goals, such as "keeper of parental morality, daytime babysitter, organizer of the PTA, and depository of young potential workers in order to keep the job market clear" (p. 409). Further, McIntire believes that schools often set convenient goals regardless of students' needs. For example, talking may be prohibited, even though social and verbal skills are important. Conformity may be required, not only with regard to clothes and conduct but also in the intellectual area. Discussions of controversial issues may therefore be avoided.

The question of personal versus institutional goals is often not dealt with explicitly by educators. In considering your own school policies and procedures, you may find that certain rules effectively stifle individual goal-setting and independent thinking. However, most educators would deny that such a situation was intended when the rules were proposed. A similar situation may also occur in the classroom. For example, do you tend to steer away from controversial discussion topics? Do you fail to solicit students' input regarding classroom rules and topics to be discussed? Have you ever asked students what they would like to accomplish during the school year? Reducing the conflict between institutional and individual goals may result in increased goal attainment for all.

Guidelines for Goal Setting.   The question of who should set educational and behavorial goals for students is a controversial one. Traditionally, adults have set the goals. And adults, unless they are incapacitated or otherwise incapable, have been allowed to make the decisions about what to do with their own lives. It has generally been accepted that individuals will be adequately able to set personal goals when they reach adulthood, but this assumption may be erroneous for many individuals. McIntire presents the thesis that goals are best set after individuals have been taught how to set goals. Skills felt to be necessary for the self-selection of goals include: being able to recognize and evaluate alternatives, being able to anticipate future consequences, and being able to assess accurately one's current behavior. We also believe that pinpointing desired behaviors, teaching, and modeling goal-setting behavior are crucial to helping students learn to set appropriate goals, and, as you would gather from the chapter on self-management, we believe most students are capable of much more self-direction than has previously been thought possible. Allowing students the freedom to determine some of their own goals and manage their own lives should reduce the likelihood that behavior management techniques will be used merely to enforce non-meaningful goals and conformity.

Conformity Versus Creativity.   The issue of student conformity versus independent behavior has not been satisfactorily resolved for many educators. Is a student being molded into a conforming adult when he is expected to sit quietly and follow class rules, but is also encouraged to think independently on controversial issues and to pursue research related to his areas of interest? We believe that stimulating ideas can be presented and independent thinking skills can be established at the same time students are conforming to classroom rules. Few students who sit quietly in class behave in

"It might help if we stopped referring to the faculty as 'us' and the students as 'them.'"

the same manner in other settings, such as the home or skating rink. In fact, similar behavior would be expected to occur only to the extent that the non-classroom setting resembled the classroom situation and to the extent that the same types of behavior were reinforced.

We are not saying that students should be shaped into docile beings who accept any rule without protest. We feel that students should be taught to discriminate between appropriate or inappropriate behaviors for a particular setting. The primary emphasis in the classroom should be on learning and thinking. Behavior requirements should be developed in accordance with the type of skill being taught. Rules for rules' sake should be avoided.

Another issue that may arise with regard to changing behavior concerns the shy, withdrawn child. Most teachers feel that shyness is an undesirable state and that the child should be helped to become more outgoing. Other teachers argue that many creative individuals are shy and withdrawn and thus one should never attempt to change this behavior. The question becomes that of whether the use of behavior management techniques to induce outgoing behavior in shy individuals stifles creativity.

Many creative individuals tend to be shy and reclusive. However, there are also scores of shy people who will never become creative geniuses. By their demeanor, it is apparent that many shy, withdrawn people are desperately unhappy. Through use of positive behavior management techniques, a shy child may be helped to experience success in social relationships and become a "happier" individual. We do not believe that it is necessary for a child to be unhappy and withdrawn for him to be creative. Furthermore, if solitary behavior is more satisfying to a child than is interacting with others, then he will probably fail to respond to attempts to change his behavior.

Ethical Issues: Behavior Change Methodology

Ethical considerations related to classroom management often involve the methodology employed to effect the change. Questions have been raised regarding the use of both positive and negative techniques. These questions are important and deserve serious consideration in any discussion of behavior change methodology. A teacher who has ethical reservations about the use of a particular behavior change technique will not be apt to use it in the classroom. We will discuss some of the issues that have been raised concerning both positive and negative techniques. A careful perusal of these issues should aid you in making decisions regarding the metholology you are willing to use in your classroom.

Ethical Considerations Related to Positive Behavior Change Techniques

Positive behavior management techniques include those methods discussed in detail in Chapter Four. Essentially, the process involves providing a reward or payoff, which may be social, tangible, or an activity, when a student exhibits desired behavior. What is necessary is that the student perform the desired behavior in order to earn the reward. An ethical question that has arisen regarding the use of positive reinforcement to change behavior has been concerned with the application of tangible reinforcers. Can the use of tangible rewards to change or maintain behavior be equated with bribery?

O'Leary, Poulas, and Devine (1972) discuss in detail eleven major objections that have been raised against the use of tangible reinforcers to change behavior. These include concerns about whether the recipient of tangible rewards will be taught greed, whether a child will be taught to be bad because he is rewarded when he is good, whether receiving tangible rewards teaches recipients to use tangibles to control others, and whether reward systems teach self-doubt by implying through "if-then" statements that one doubts the ability of the individual to perform the behavior. Further concerns have been expressed in regard to the dispenser of token reinforcement. Will he come to rely on this form of behavior control and fail to develop other methods? Concern has also been focused on individuals who are not rewarded for displaying a particular behavior. Will people who observe others being rewarded for behaving appropriately behave inappropriately in order to be offered rewards for desirable behavior? Additional questions relate to the duration of behavior change achieved via tangible reinforcement and to the effect of rewarding certain behaviors on other behaviors that are not rewarded. A final objection suggests that tangible reinforcement may interfere with learning.

Reinforcement Versus Bribery.   In considering this question, it becomes apparent that different standards are applied to children than to adults. For example, as employed adults, we are presently receiving a payoff for performing the duties outlined in our job descriptions. Most of us would be highly unlikely to continue if financial remuneration were suddenly discontinued. Are our employers bribing us to work? Or, to ask a more personal question, are you being bribed to teach? Most of us would answer a resounding "No." We feel that we are making honest and important contributions through our work. On the other hand, outlining desired behaviors for a child (e.g., making a bed, picking up toys, completing homework, bringing books to class), and providing a tangible reward contingent on the desired behaviors is often regarded as bribery. Expectations for children are sometimes higher than for adults. Just as work is usually not intrinsically rewarding enough for us to continue when external support (i.e., the paycheck) is withdrawn, so certain behaviors required of children may not be inherently reinforcing. External support may be required until the behavior is well established and is being maintained by intrinsic reinforcement. For example, a child may initially keep a neat room and take a daily bath without protest only when allowed to earn points or tokens to exchange for money or toys. Later, the pride of having a neat room and the self satisfaction that accompanies a well-groomed body may be sufficient to maintain these behaviors.

Apparently, the concept of bribery remains unclear for many people. When rewards are made contingent on desired behavior, the process is sometimes equated with bribery. The primary definition of a bribe agrees with this view only to the extent that an individual in a position of trust is induced to commit illegal or corrupt acts. Careful study of the classroom research using tangible reinforcers indicates that the procedure has been used to induce appropriate academic and social behavior in the research subjects. No studies can be found in which illegal and corrupt acts receive a payoff. Thus, tangible rewards for appropriate behavior cannot be considered bribes in the primary sense of the word. The secondary definition of a bribe, "something that serves to induce or influence," is more consistent with the use of tangible rewards in the home or classroom. Using the term in this very general sense also means that most of us are bribed daily.

Effects of Tangible Rewards on Recipients. The effects of receiving tangible rewards contingent on performing a specified behavior can be considerable. On the positive side, the receiver will probably emit the desired behaviors, and thus may be able to learn new skills and to improve his functioning in the environment. On the negative side, the possibility that greed may inadvertantly be taught and that the receiver may imitate the dispenser in attempting to control others through this method must be considered. Some receivers may attempt to manipulate the dispenser by demanding rewards for the performance of additional behaviors. For these reasons, tangible reinforcers should be used only when social or activity rewards are ineffective. In such a case, they should be paired with non-tangible items (e.g., praise) in an attempt to develop other reinforcing events. The individual should gradually be phased on to a more naturalistic system. Fortunately, as people learn to perform new skills, the new behaviors often become reinforcing in their own right, and extrinsic rewards are no longer required for the maintenance of the behavior.

The possibility that a person will be taught to be bad by being rewarded for being good increases when rewards are not offered until he engages in undesirable behavior.

AN UNEXPECTED RESULT
Susie, a fourth grader, liked to walk about the room and talk to her peers. Whenever she did this, her teacher, Mrs. Brewster, often responded by saying "Sit down, Susie, and I'll let you . . . ."

The offending behavior invariably ceased at that time. However, Susie was observed to get up more and more frequently. At one point she asked Mrs. Brewster "If I don't talk to Brenda, will you let me . . .?

Mrs. Brewster was aghast at Susie's presumptiveness. Then she realized that her method of applying positive reinforcement might be teaching Susie to behave badly in order to receive additional privileges. She therefore spelled out the contingencies in advance for all the children and refrained from offering a special reward when a child was observed to be misbehaving. With the contingencies made clear and with consistency in implementing the program, no other problems were encountered.

In the situation described above, the student was essentially taught to misbehave in order to receive a reward. To prevent such an occurrence, contingencies should be spelled out in advance and rewards should be offered only when an individual is behaving appropriately. If-then statements ("If you'll stop talking, then you may have some bubble gum") contribute to the problem. O'Leary, Poulas, and Devine contend that continued use of if-then statements, even for the development of positive skills, may be aversive to the recipient, and suggest that the use of these statements be minimized as much as possible.

Effects of Tangible Rewards on Dispensers.   The successful use of tangible reinforcement may also have an effect on the dispenser of the rewards. Certainly, finding that one can control another person's behavior through use of these procedures is potentially reinforcing. It is important, then, that individuals who administer behavior change programs gradually phase out tangible rewards in favor of social reinforcement. Perhaps teachers should think of tangible rewards only as a temporary tool, and, perhaps, they should consider a self-monitoring program to determine the extent to which their classroom behavior change program continues to rely on tangible reinforcement. No teacher wants to fall into the trap of using tangible rewards simply because he is getting reinforced by the system. As with all classroom management systems, the ultimate aim is to help the students.

Effects of Tangible Rewards on Non-Rewarded Individuals.   The effects of giving tangible rewards to one person and not to others must also be considered. When children who are not rewarded see one or more of their peers receiving rewards for performing a particular behavior, they may feel that the situation is unfair.

REINFORCING NEAT BEHAVIOR

Jerry was a chronically messy student. Mr. Delano decided to use a token program to increase neat behavior. Thus, he instituted a desk check three times a day, and awarded tokens when Jerry's desk met his criteria for neatness. The tokens were exchangeable for money to operate a coke machine. Jerry's messy behavior improved rapidly, and he became very proud of his neat desk. To Mr. Delano's suprise, however, other students began to complain bitterly about not receiving tokens for their clean desks. In two weeks, messy desks began to proliferate in the classroom. What appeared to be a successful behavior change program had degenerated into an unworkable situation.

In the above situation, all of the students originally did not require a tangible reward for keeping a neat desk. However, the fact that one child was receiving rewards for performing this behavior eventually became unacceptable to the other students. We would be in much the same situation if we worked overtime without pay only to discover that one of our colleagues received pay for the same service. Williams and Anandam (1973) suggest that this type of problem can be circumvented in the classroom by contracting with all of the students. Under a contract, students may be allowed to pursue independent alternatives and still receive a reward. Thus, one individual is not singled out for special attention.

Effects of Non-Natural Rewards. In general, behaviors supported by reinforcers that are unnatural to the situation (e.g., tokens) may extinguish when the external support is withdrawn. A teacher who proposes using tangible reinforcement must make an effort to develop more natural reinforcers (e.g., social attention) if the behavior change is to be of long duration. O'Leary, Poulas, and Devine suggest that the use of tokens may be inadvisable if the program is of short duration, because of the possibility that tokens may represent a distraction, and thus interfere with learning. This effect is not felt to hold when the program continues for a long period of time.

Ethical Considerations Related to Negative
Behavior Change Techniques

Just as ethical questions have been raised regarding the use of certain positive behavior change techniques, so questions have arisen regarding use of negative techniques for such change. Two negative means, in particular, have traditionally been accepted and used frequently to control behavior in the classroom: criticism and corporal punishment. During the past ten years, two additional methods have been employed with increasing frequency: time out and response cost. We have already discussed the use of these strategies in Chapter Five, but we want to reconsider them in this chapter, primarily in light of the ethical and legal questions they pose for teachers. The major ethical issue to be raised with regard to negative means of behavior change questions is whether it should be employed at all. Is it wrong to punish a child? The answer to this question involves a value judgment that we cannot decide for you. However, we will discuss some of the ethical issues that should be taken into account when negative means of behavior change are considered for use in the classroom.

Corporal punishment. Corporal punishment has been used frequently in the past as a means of changing students' behavior. Yet, the question pertaining to who will decide what behaviors should be changed is seldom asked when it is considered. Perhaps the relative long-term ineffectiveness of this technique has resulted in complacency regarding this matter. Further, corporal punishment is often employed without prior planning. Regardless of the frequency of application, the question pertaining to the purpose of behavior change should apply here. A teacher who paddles a child for talking during class periods is communicating her values loudly and clearly. A teacher who spanks a child who talks back is publishing a belief that children should show respect for those in authority.

Educators in school districts that allow corporal punishment must ask whether an individual has a right to inflict pain on another human being. Certainly, most of us refrain from doing so on an adult. In the case of a child, however, physical pain is often inflicted with the verbal justification that the child will "learn to do better" or that the whipping is administered for the "good of the child." One can only speculate about the long-range effects of using physical punishment. As pointed out in Chapter Five, it is known that the punisher is modeling aggressive behavior for the child, and children tend to imitate aggressive behavior that they have seen modeled. Children who are abused by their parents often grow up to abuse their own children. Furthermore, the use of corporal punishment may engender strong emotional reactions in the recipient. The possibility thus arises that children who are repeatedly physically punished may suffer emotional problems. When one is made to feel inconsequential, one's self-esteem cannot help but be lowered.

As we just mentioned, adults tend to refrain from physically striking adults. However, inflicting pain on others seems to continue in a different form. Criticism, sarcasm, and verbal downgrading of others results in emotional pain for the recipient. Is it possible that the negative events that are suffered in childhood are imitated in perhaps a different and more acceptable form in adulthood?

Additional considerations related to the use of corporal punishment in school districts where it is legally sanctioned included the following questions: Is this child entitled to the same rights as adults? What am I teaching this child by spanking him? Will the child refrain from performing the deviant behavior, or will he learn that one can do as one pleases when big enough to exert power over others? Emotionally, how will this child react to paddling? Will he develop a dislike for the teacher? And even more serious, how can we be sure that emotional behaviors that are engendered by physical punishment will not generalize to the school itself? Will the child begin to dislike coming to school? Behavior theory would postulate that repeated pairing of physical punishment and school could result in such a reaction. No conscientious teacher can say that this situation would be desirable.

Criticism. Criticism represents a commonly accepted method for changing behavior, but one seldom hears ethical questions raised about it. Nevertheless, criticism can be used in various ways, but not all teachers and parents are constructive in their approach. For example, criticism may be employed without thought as to the overall effect it can have on the recipient. It is not unusual to hear a teacher say "John is a lazy child. He could do better if he tried" or "Mary, you are a sloppy writer. You must learn to be neater." Most individuals who attempt to change behavior through criticism are quick to point out that only "constructive" criticism is used. The term "constructive criticism," however, is often used to cover any criticism they might employ. After all, who likes to think that he is using destructive criticism?

Ginott (1965) defined constructive criticism as criticism that is confined to the target behavior and that omits negative remarks about personality. For example, a teacher might say "Mary, papers are easier to read when they are neatly copied." Such a statement provides information regarding the task to be completed, and it casts no aspersions on the recipient. Or, perhaps, a teacher might say, "John, in order to complete your arithmetic assignments on time, it will be necessary for you to work during study time rather than look at a comic book." This statement tells John what is necessary, but does not imply that he is lazy. In particular, one should refrain from using derogatory adjectives when pointing out the shortcomings of others. According to Ginott, when parents call their child clumsy or stupid, the result is a chain of reactions that makes both the child and the parents miserable. When a child is repeatedly described in derogatory terms, he begins to believe these things about himself, and begins to behave in a manner that is consistent with these beliefs. In order to use criticism in a constructive manner, teachers should focus on the task to be done, avoid attacking the personality of the recipient, and avoid derogatory comments. And teachers should give criticism quietly, limit it to the situation at hand, and be brief with their remarks. Our opinion is that destructive criticism is always unethical and uncalled for. How do you view such criticism?

Time Out.   Time out, as you will recall from Chapter Five, is a behavior control technique that involves removing an individual from a reinforcing situation and placing him in a situation that does not provide rewards. Unfortunately, it is sometimes used with abandon, thus taking on the characteristics of an aversive technique. Situations have been described in which children or adults were isolated for hours or placed in dark or locked rooms. When time out is applied in a harsh fashion, individuals may be deprived not only of basic social contact but also of basic human needs for long periods of time. In addition, the person's legal rights may be violated. Intense frustration and other emotional reactions may be associated with the process. As with any negative behavior control technique, care must be taken that an inhumane approach is not used. Time out should be employed only when one has a basic understanding of the method and its application. Arrangements should be made for continual monitoring of any behavior change program incorporating time out in order to insure that the method is not abused.

Response Cost.   You will remember from earlier discussions that the classroom use of response costs usually involves the loss of a privilege or perhaps points toward a grade. The technique appears to be a reasonable method for controlling behavior when used properly. For example, care should be taken that minor infractions of the rules do not result in extreme penalties. Failure to turn in homework on Tuesday should not result in loss of enough points to fail a student for the week. The fine or cost should be appropriate to the "crime." Earning an excessive fine on Monday would, no doubt, remove incentive for completing assignments for the remainder of the week. On the other hand, a very minor fine may result in no behavior change. Thus, a teacher must attempt to set an optimal and fair penalty when using this technique.

It is especially important that the cost of misbehaving be specified in advance. The technique should not suddenly be applied at the whim of a teacher. If students are to learn to control their own behavior, they must learn to appreciate in advance the consequences of performing specified behaviors. Erratic application of behavior control techniques does not always afford them this opportunity.

The response cost technique can be applied on a group basis as well as on an individual basis. Some teachers choose to use the procedure with entire classes.

FAIR OR UNFAIR?

Mr. Bluefield, a ninth grade shop teacher, continually had a problem with students' being tardy to his sixth period class. He decided that the problem would be solved only if he imposed a stiff penalty for tardiness. Accordingly, he announced that each time a student was late, the entire class would be denied the privilege of being dismissed five minutes earlier to board school buses. Since the problem was confined to two or three students who were chronically late, the rest of the students complained bitterly about the contingencies. As expected, group pressure was applied to the boys, and the situation improved somewhat. However, tardiness was not completely eliminated, and the class as a whole continued to lose occasionally the special privilege of boarding the bus early. It was circulated through the student grapevine that Mr. Bluefield was an unfair teacher.

The application of the response cost technique on a group contingent basis raises questions of an ethical nature. Is it fair to penalize several children for the misbehavior of one child?

Should group pressure be applied in changing an individual student's behavior? The group contingent response cost technique is generally a powerful one for changing behavior. However, we believe that response cost for an entire group should be considered a supplementary means of behavior control, to be used only when the behavior of several students need to be changed at the same time. Further, group contingent programs should be of short duration. In the long-run, each student should be required to deal with the consequences of his own behavior. Is it right to ask a student to accept indefinitely the consequences of peers' behavior?

Legal Issues: Students' Rights

In the past, teachers and principals considered it their job to maintain discipline and to teach in the way they saw fit. Little attention was given to the rights of students or to the techniques used to maintain classroom control. This situation has changed in recent years. School personnel must now be aware of the legal implications of techniques used in the classroom. In fact, many teachers consider it prudent to carry some type of malpractice insurance in the event that legal problems arise over something that has happened in the classroom. Students' rights and due process are terms that have been added to the vocabulary of most educators. Parents and students now realize that there are definite limits to the authority that teachers and principals can exercise. We will discuss some of the issues now facing teachers with regard to legal aspects of behavior control. It is important to be aware of the current status of these issues. It is equally important to be aware that legal interpretations may change and that new issues may arise, which can have legal implications for teachers.

Due Process

The fifth amendment to the Constitution provides in part that "No person shall be ... deprived of life, liberty, or property, without due process of law." The fourteenth amendment further states " ... Nor shall any State deprive any person of life, liberty or property, without due process of law; nor deny to any person within its jurisdiction the equal protection of the laws." Basically, due process has been interpreted to require that prior notice of prohibited behavior be provided. In addition, notification of when the penalty is to be applied for some suspected reason must also be given (Martin, 1975). In the past, students have not always been accorded the privilege of due process, with the result that many have been expelled without adequate hearings, or have been required to accept severe and unfair treatment. Court decisions (Gault, 1967; Goss and Lopez, 1975) within the past decade have provided new guidelines regarding the interpretation of these clauses as they apply to children. Basically, the Gault case made it clear that the rights guaranteed by the Constitution are not for adults alone. The Goss and Lopez case held that students facing suspensions from school are entitled to due process under the law. The court further held that students have a right to know the charges against them and be given an opportunity to respond to them. Thus, the idea that children have basic rights has now been made clear by the courts. Teachers and school administrators can no longer overlook this aspect of law when making decisions pertaining to behavior control. Ritchie (1973) suggested the following guidelines that still remain appropriate: (1) Rules and procedures for dealing with conflicts between school and student should be nonadversary in nature and design. (2) Procedures relating to serious student-school conflicts that could result in suspension or expulsion of a student should include due process exemplified by prior knowledge of the behavior that is required or prohibited, prior notification that the proposed penalty is to be imposed and the specific reason for imposing the penalty, opportunity for a hearing regarding the charges, and a fair decision.

Equal Protection

Individuals are not only entitled to due process of law but also to equal protection by the law. Martin (1975) interprets equal protection to mean that "a state agency cannot treat one group substantially differently from other groups entitled to the same treatment!"

EDUCATION: A RIGHT OF ALL CITIZENS

Marian, a girl of normal intelligence, was a victim of cerebral palsy, which limited her ability to engage in all the activities of children her age. In order for her to be successful in school, special arrangements were necessary. At times, she had seizures that required attention from her caretaker. Thus, very early in her school career, teachers suggested to her parents that she did not fit in and that it would be best if she were not sent to school. Her parents were unwilling to accept this suggestion, feeling that their daughter was entitled to the same basic education as were non-handicapped children. However, they were unsuccessful in obtaining educational training for Marian. Now, twenty years later, their dream for their daughter has become a reality for many other handicapped children.

Fortunately, the equal protection clause covers the handicapped. In addition, identifiable groups (e.g., blacks, Spanish-speaking, females) cannot be singled out for treatment different from that received by other students. Martin suggests that one should examine a chosen intervention strategy to determine whether it incorporates different treatment for one discernible group. If so, it should be changed. In addition, one should make sure that any discernible group of people is not excluded from the treatment without justification.

Legal Issues: Behavior Change Techniques

Behavior change techniques should be scrutinized to detect legal implications that may be related to their use or misuse. Improperly applied, some techniques may result in curtailment of basic student rights. Due process and equal protection may not be afforded when the technique is used. This can happen with positive reward systems as well as with negative approaches, such as corporal punishment and time out.

Positive Reward Systems

Positive behavior management techniques have been fully described in previous chapters, and ethical aspects related to reward systems have been discussed in this chapter. An additional consideration pertaining to positive rewards may have legal implications. Basically, one should insure that students are not deprived of items to which they are entitled as a right. For example, John may certainly be motivated to earn the privilege of eating his lunch. However, the right to eat is basic, and manipulation of a right such as this can have legal implications. It is better that he be allowed to earn a bag of potato chips as an extra treat and that his basic meal be non-contingent on a specific behavior. To quote Martin (p. 126) "If the program leads to a severe change in status or if personal property is taken away and used as a reward to be earned, it may violate the fifth amendment." Therefore, teachers should question the often-practiced confiscation of student property that is to be returned when the student has met a certain behavioral or academic standard.

Time Out

As we stated earlier, time out has often been used inappropriately. Martin, in discussing this technique, points out the importance of providing for due process (e.g., notice of intent to discipline, allowance of a period of time to prepare a defense, and a hearing) when isolation is imposed for disciplinary reasons. Fortunately, very few teachers consider long periods of isolation to be necessary motivators of student behavior. But what of short periods in a time out room? Martin (p. 86) suggests that if one can assure that "any administration of time out as a motivating technique will not stretch to an hour or otherwise represent a substantial deprivation of liberty, then it might be used. If you cannot make that guarantee, then it should not even be attempted." Any educator who proposes to use time out should be aware of the legal ramifications pertaining to its use. Certainly, if the technique cannot be applied appropriately, it should not be used at all.

Corporal Punishment

The use of physical punishment raises not only ethical questions; legal implications may also arise from its use or misuse. A recent Supreme Court ruling in *Baker* vs. *Owen* (1975) upheld a lower court opinion that schools have a right to use corporal punishment, under state law, even though the parents may object. In accordance with this ruling, procedural safeguards require giving prior warning that certain behaviors will result in corporal punishment, arranging for another school official to witness the punishment, telling the witness, beforehand and in the student's presence, the reason for the punishment, and providing parents who request an explanation a written statement detailing the reasons for the punishment and the name of the witness.

Do not assume from the above-mentioned case that all teachers have a right to use corporal punishment. This is not the situation. At least three states—Maryland, Massachusetts, and New Jersey—presently prohibit it. And even in states where corporal punishment is not explicitly prohibited by state law, local ordinances may prohibit its use. Therefore, we suggest that you inquire about the laws in your state and school district before contemplating the use of physical punishment. Remember, too, that although you may be permitted to use physical punishment, you cannot apply it indiscriminately. You should be aware that it is becoming increasingly common for parents to turn to the courts for redress in cases where they feel their child has been wronged or has been administered cruel and unusual punishment.

Legal Issues: Accountability

Undoubtedly, teachers and other school personnel will eventually have to become accountable for making changes in behavior. Unfortunately, the goals of many schools and teachers are so elusive as to make accountability impossible. For example, how does one measure whether a second grader has learned to become a good citizen? In order to determine whether teachers are actually fulfilling their expected and remunerated roles, job descriptions should be clear and precise. Exactly what is expected of you as a teacher? If a job description is not offered, sit down with your supervisor and ask for one. Then, there will be a yardstick by which to measure whether you are fulfilling your job expectations. Teaching without a goal is like driving without a destination. How does one know when the goal is reached? Conceivably the public will more and more hold educators accountable for making specific changes in students' behavior. Setting precise goals, and documenting students' progress, will not only assist in teaching but can also provide information regarding accountability.

Summary

This chapter focused on ethical and legal implications related to the use of behavior management techniques in the classroom. Specific ethical questions concerned with behavior change include whether behavior management techniques should be used to induce conformity, who should make the decisions regarding the behaviors to be changed, and whether changing shy, withdrawn behavior stifles creativity. Questions pertaining to positive behavior change methodology include whether it is ethical to use tangible rewards, whether a reward procedure teaches undesirable values, and whether tangible reinforcement is equal to bribery. Ethical questions arising from the use of negative behavior change techniques were seen to revolve around corporal punishment, criticism, time out, and response cost. Problems related to the use of these techniques were discussed.

The discussion of legal implications related to the use of behavior management techniques stressed the importance of educators' becoming aware of new developments in this area. Due process, equal protection under the law, and accountability represent concepts that should be meaningful to every educator. Specific problems that could be encountered with the use of reward systems and time out were delineated. The 1975 Supreme Court decision pertaining to corporal punishment was discussed, and educators were cautioned to set school policies that are harmonious with existing laws and court rulings. Diligence in complying with these policies was also stressed.

Suggested Projects

1. Discuss how having students work quietly at their desks could be a benefit to them and how such a rule, if carried to an extreme, could be detrimental.
2. Describe why students might fail to question goals that have been set for them by others. How could class meetings and/or teacher verbal reinforcement be used to help students be more willing to express their own ideas?
3. Tell how you could reinforce behaviors that you consider to be creative?
4. Develop a procedure for informing parents regarding your plans for using reinforcement programs in the classroom. How will you deal with their questions pertaining to the ethics of classroom management?
5. A colleague tells you that Bob and Phyllis have been passing notes in his class. He says that he plans to seize the next note and is considering reading it before the entire class. He wants your advice. Do you see any ethical or legal problems with his plan?
6. Invite a lawyer who is knowledgeable about school law to attend a faculty meeting or an in-service training session. Ask for current information regarding classroom management techniques and other issues related to teaching.

REFERENCES

Ginott, H. G. *Between parent and child.* New York: The Macmillan Company, 1965.

Martin, R. *Legal challenges to behavior modification.* Champaign, Illinois: Research Press, 1975.

McIntire, R. W. "Guidelines for using behavior modification in education." In R. Ulrich, T. Stachnik and J. Mabry (Eds.) *Control of human behavior.* Glenview, Illinois: Scott, Foresman Company, 1974.

O'Leary, K. D.; Poulos, R. W.; and Devine, V. T. "Tangible reinforcers, bonuses or bribes?" *Journal of Consulting and Clinical Psychology* 38 (1972): 1–8.

Ritchie, R. M. "Due process and the principal." *Phi Delta Kappan* 54 (1973): 697–98.

Williams, R. L., and Anandam, K. *Cooperative classroom management.* Columbus, Ohio: Charles E. Merrill Publishing Company, 1973.

Winett, R. A., and Winkler, R. C. "Current behavior modification in the classroom: be still, be quiet, be docile." *Journal of Applied Behavior Analysis* 5 (1972): 499–504.

CHAPTER NINE

PUTTING IT ALL TOGETHER

As the preceding chapters have indicated, establishing effective classroom discipline is no simple matter. Many variables operate in every classroom, making it impossible to provide a single answer that can be universally applied. Furthermore, effective classroom management seldom results from making just *one* change in the classroom. Often the successful approach requires the careful orchestration of many factors. Of course, knowledge and competency with regard to specific disciplinary techniques are important. Just as important is the ability to "put it all together." The effective teacher is one who is able to see each situation in an objective perspective and to change as many aspects of the situation as is required to establish and maintain an optimal learning environment. In this chapter, we want to look at how suggestions in the previous chapters can be integrated to help with the establishment of effective classroom management. We will apply our suggestions to the solution of a common classroom problem. Then we will give you the opportunity to see how well you can do with specific problems.

General Review

The text began with the theme that influencing students' behavior in a positive direction is what classroom management is all about (Chapter One). Attention was then directed to how teacher attitudes can make a substantial difference in whether a classroom environment is seen as being positive or negative by the students (Chapter Two). We pointed out that the attitudes that a teacher holds toward students as well as toward himself affect his perception of classroom incidents, and, to a large extent, determine whether each situation is viewed as troublesome or trivial. We noted that the ability of teachers to have a favorable and lasting influence on students is enhanced to the extent that they are able to emphasize, accept, and display genuine feelings toward others. Being able to admit mistakes, listening to what students have to say, looking for positive qualities in students, and responding positively to students were recognized as procedures that could go a long way in increasing genuine communication. Positive feelings about oneself were also recognized as being representative of positive attitudes towards others.

While we recognized the value of positive attitudes toward both students and oneself, we stressed that attitudes *alone* cannot be expected to prevent or solve all classroom management problems. The way teachers organize the classroom environment was seen as having a profound effect on classroom behaviors. We cautioned that desired behaviors often must be prompted (Chapter Three). And we emphasized that students should be told what is expected of them, because rules cannot be followed if they have only been assumed by the teacher and have never been made explicit for the student. We also stressed that instructions should be given in a clear and simple manner, a setting that is conducive to learning should be provided, appropriate materials should be used, and critical behaviors modeled for the students.

After stressing the importance of setting the stage for desired student behaviors, attention was directed at the significance of properly managing the consequences of student behavior (Chapter Four). We indicated that in order to establish and maintain effective classroom control, teachers must arrange to make desired behavior pay. Social rewards (e.g., teacher praise) were discussed as potential payoffs for most students. However, the necessity for providing a variety of rewards to meet the needs of every student was also recognized. You will remember that all payoffs must be rewarding to the recipient, and not just to the dispenser of the reward. Although a number of specific suggestions were offered regarding the proper control of consequences, the overall theme on the subject was: focusing on the positive, rather than the negative, aspects of student behaviors can exert a strong influence on the emotional climate and productivity of a classroom.

As we noted earlier, exhibiting positive attitudes, setting the stage for desired behaviors, and positively reinforcing appropriate behaviors can combine to prevent most of the problems that teachers encounter. As a matter of fact, effective classroom management *requires* that these conditions exist. But, as you will recall from previous chapters, *all* problems cannot be prevented. Teachers need strategies for dealing with excessive behaviors that will occur despite preventive efforts (Chapter Five). Alternative strategies identified for handling such problems included: altering setting events, reinforcing behaviors incompatible with inappropriate behaviors, using appropriate peer models, providing for stimulus satiation, and extinction. Mildly punitive techniques, such as soft reprimands, time out, response cost, and overcorrection, were also discussed.

We also suggested that virtually every teacher will face problems that go beyond his level of expertise (Chapter Six). We stressed the importance of recognizing problems that imply the need for referral. And, we asked that a working relationship be established with resource persons in the school and in the community. The need for cooperative efforts between the school and the home was emphasized. Throughout, the implication was that no one can solve all problems alone. We have always felt that seeking needed assistance from others is a sign of maturity—not of weakness.

We recommended that student involvement, too, play a major role in effective classroom management (Chapter Seven). The desire of most students for independence becomes especially acute as they grow older. Students, like most of us, like to feel they have a measure of control over what happens to them in daily life. Further, students are expected to manage their own lives after they finish school. So we discussed a number of techniques that are frequently used in helping others achieve a greater degree of self-control. These included: self-recording, control of setting events, management of consequences, self-verbalizations, and behavioral contracting. The emphasis was on a planned program for giving students more responsibility for directing their lives as they demonstrate great self-management abilities.

Finally, attention was given to the ethical and legal problems of classroom management (Chapter Eight). While specific classroom management techniques may be combined to produce changes in student behaviors, we realized that teachers often use different techniques because of their beliefs about right and wrong. Therefore, we asked that a careful examination of all classroom management practices be made to determine whether those techniques could meet the highest ethical standards, as well as correspond to all legal requirements. The special attention to ethical and legal issues underscored our own belief that only classroom control that recognizes the rights and dignity of every person can ultimately accomplish the high goal of enriching the lives of students and teachers.

Approaching Actual Problems

Apparently, from what has been said thus far, we believe effective classroom management involves some elements from each of the preceding chapters. Indeed, we believe Chapters Two through Eight constitute a workable model for managing most classroom problems. We are not saying that our format is the only one to follow. Far from it. Few problems can be permanently resolved without implementing the salient points in each of the chapters. Naturally, some problems will involve greater emphasis on one or more of these points than others. Nonetheless, each ought to be considered and controlled when essential to a problem's solution. With this format as a model, let us look at how a specific classroom problem might be solved. We will make a number of suggestions from each chapter. You can use those that seem most appropriate for you and your students.

Problem: Defiance[1]

Mrs. Martin, a second-year teacher, had been experiencing increasing difficulties with a number of her eighth grade students. Early in the year she seemed to get along with them. They seemed anxious to please her. Later on, though, she noticed that the boys were becoming less compliant to her requests. They would murmur among themselves, exchange glances, and take their time about doing what Mrs. Martin asked. Sometimes students would even ignore her, acting as though they had not heard her. Mrs.

---

[1]Teachers tell us that defiance is one of the most widespread problems in the schools. It often takes the form of impoliteness, refusing to do as told, and cursing the teacher.

Martin had initially avoided taking any action, hoping the problem would go away. However, she realized something had to be done when one of her students remarked, "I'm not going to do it," after being asked to stop talking. Assume you are the teacher. What can be done?

Examine personal attitudes. Regardless of whether the problem is student defiance or another classroom management difficulty, you will always want to examine your own attitudes to determine if they may be contributing to the problem. This step is especially critical when the problem involves disagreements between yourself and a student. Perhaps a change in your own attitude can steer student-teacher relationships in a positive direction. Consideration of the following questions may provide useful information with regard to how teacher attitudes influence student defiance:

1. *Attitudes toward others.*   Has the student done something in the past to make you more "watchful" of him? Could you be expecting the worst as far as the student is concerned? Do you believe that a teacher should show students who is boss? As a result, do you dare students to defy you? Have you, perhaps unconsciously, set up situations that will increase the probability that confrontative behavior will materialize?
2. *Attitudes toward self.*   How does it make you feel when a student refuses to comply with your requests? Are you afraid of appearing weak if compromise is allowed? Do you feel that respect for a teacher will be lower if he admits to making a mistake? How do you think other people will view you if they find out that a student has successfully defied you?

After examining your own attitudes, you may find that the problem is being prompted or exaggerated by your own actions. If so, perhaps one or more of the following suggestions would be among those you should implement:

1. Demonstrate a willingness to admit mistakes. Your credibility will be increased, and it is more likely that students will consider your requests worthy of compliance.
2. Use an indirect approach when dealing with defiant students. Respond to the feelings behind their overt behavior. (Remember our comments on listening to others.)

3. Attempt to establish a personal relationship with your students. Knowing something good about each student and communicating it can demonstrate that you care about each person in your class. Direct defiance of your authority is less likely if students feel you are interested in them.
4. Put misbehavior in perspective. Students who defy your authority may have little against you personally. Realizing this may help you respond more calmly.
5. Treat all students equally. Do not require compliance from some students while other students are not required to comply with the same request or rules.

Set the stage for desirable behavior.   You must also be cognizant of the environment you are providing. When a problem like defiance arises, you will want to ask, "Does the environment in my class prompt good behavior?" In other words, is the stage set for desirable behavior? Remember, by providing an environment that fosters desirable behavior, you will invariably minimize problem behavior. Thus, based on the ideas presented in Chapter Three, we offer the following suggestions for prompting cooperation:

1. Set up explicit classroom rules. If the rules are vague, the students may find a technical loophole for defying you.
2. Allow students to help make the rules. They are less likely to break a rule they have helped make.
3. Make sure you do not give instructions that are beyond a student's capacity to follow. Defiance can sometimes be a result of being frustrated over complex instructions.
4. Be alert to minor indicators that defiance may be brewing. Try to deal with the problem before major defiance occurs.
5. Make sure that your requests are within students' capacity to perform. Students will often defy a teacher and suffer the consequences rather than lose face with peers because they are unable to do what is asked of them.
6. Consider developing a unit dealing with the idea of authority. Help students develop positive reasons for cooperating in the classroom.
7. Arrange to have students who reliably cooperate with requests serve as appropriate models by requesting and rein-

forcing cooperative behaviors in the presence of the other students.

8. Model the behaviors you expect. That is, tell students why you are following certain policies yourself and demonstrate how you comply. You should also avoid behaving in aggressive ways.

9. Closely related to modeling appropriate behavior is the need to avoid giving commands that you have no authority to enforce or that you would be unable to enforce if confronted. It is better to ask students to do something than to tell them what they are going to do.

Accentuate appropriate behavior. Managing defiant behavior does not stop with attitudinal changes and the prompting of cooperation. Cooperative actions must be rewarded if they are to be maintained. Chapter Four clearly indicated what will happen when appropriate behaviors are taken for granted. Mrs. Martin's case provides a further example. It appears that she took the initial cooperative behaviors of her students for granted. The following suggestions, based on ideas in Chapter Four, are aimed at making certain that cooperative behaviors pay off for your students:

1. Make an effort to notice when students cooperate, and verbally praise this behavior.

2. Pair verbal praise with other rewards, For example, you might say, "Sam, thank you for working quietly on your algebra. You may take the remaining ten minutes of class to read your library book."

3. Make sure students understand that praise and rewards are tied to cooperative behavior. Reward immediately following acts of cooperation.

4. Occasionally reward the class as a whole when they have been diligent about following a class rule. For instance, the students might be given an extra five minutes of recess. Make sure that all of the students have followed the rule before you reward them all. Otherwise, some may be reinforced for breaking the rule.

5. When a student seldom fully cooperates, shape cooperative behavior by rewarding behaviors that approximate the goal of full cooperation. For example, if a student cooperates

with only a part of your request, reinforce this act of cooperation and work toward the goal of more complete cooperation.

Consider developing alternative strategies for temporarily suppressing "serious" problems. The preceding suggestions were aimed primarily at preventing the occurrence of student challenges to authority. As with most other problems, our belief is that the basic approach to dealing with defiance should be preventive in nature, rather than crisis-oriented. Teachers who operate with a crisis orientation usually have plenty to help keep them busy. Crisis after crisis often occurs. Teachers who use a preventive approach can avoid many of these unfortunate situations. However, as pointed out earlier, serious problems occasionally arise even in classes where desirable behavior is consistently prompted and rewarded. Certainly, Mrs. Martin cannot ignore the type of defiance that we described. She needs immediate plans for temporarily suppressing the defiance. Her temporary measures, of course, should be combined with the more long-range preventive techniques. Based on several ideas presented in Chapter Five, we offer the following suggestions:

1. Try to deal with the inappropriate behavior in private (a change in setting events). Little can be accomplished when opposing individuals are forced into a confrontation while other individuals are watching. If the student complies with your request to accompany you out of the room, try to find a place where he can sit quietly and "cool off" before you attempt to discuss the problem. This time will also allow you to make arrangements for your other students.

2. While withholding all attention for defiance is probably an unrealistic request to make of you, attention can be directed at the student's feelings and reasons for defiance rather than at the overt behavior itself. For example, you might say, "You believe I should not have asked you to stop talking at this particular moment," "You feel I have been unfair with you today." If the student in any way responds positively to your empathy, the door may be open for talking out the problem. In effect, you have started an extinction process by withholding attention for inappropriate behavior while reinforcing appropriate expressions.

3. When a teacher's authority is challenged, the problem is usually not confined to one student and the teacher. Other students in the class may also become emotionally involved even though they do not overtly act out. To avoid having students take sides and possibly reinforce defiance by directing attention to the problem, we suggest that student attention be focused on assignments. Saying, "We have work to do; this is between . . . and myself" will usually suffice. You might also consider having a group meeting at a later time to discuss how peer attention influences class behavior.

4. If a student is obstinate about staying in the class and is threatening you, it may be necessary to ask for assistance from the school administrator. However, the basic problem cannot be solved by the principal or vice-principal. The problem remains between you and the student. The principal may be required to remove the student for a temporary period (time out), but you should personally work out the problem with the student after a cooling off period has been allowed.

5. Avoid using harsh punishment or suggesting to the principal that the student be suspended. A positive approach incorporating some curtailment of privileges, but allowing a student to overcome the incident without extreme action, seems preferable. Suspension may be viewed by the disinterested student as a holiday, rather than punishment. Thus, the intended effect may not result.

Consider the need for working with others.   As you will recall from Chapter Six, teachers cannot resolve every problem by themselves. Therefore, with this specific problem, we suggest that you:

1. Consult with the school counselor or school psychologist. If the problem has been going on for some time without resolution, you may need objective analysis from another professional. You might ask the counselor, for example, to observe your interactions with the students and give you suggestions about possible changes.

2. Have a personal talk with the defiant student's parents. You could indicate that you and he are having difficulties. You could also get their suggestions for dealing with their child.

Talking with parents can avert subsequent disagreements over why they have not been advised earlier, should the problem continue.

Involve the students. No teacher can eliminate defiance without the cooperation of the students. Frequently, defiant students wish they had never challenged others, but they lack the know-how for achieving greater self-control. At other times, students may become defiant simply because they have been excluded from decision-making processes. We suggest that the students be given the opportunity to:

1. Examine the setting events and reinforcers that may be precipitating and controlling their behaviors.
2. Consider the merits of self-verbalizations. (This tactic seems extremely appropriate for helping students practice more acceptable ways of expressing themselves.)
3. Develop behavioral contracts for appropriate classroom behaviors.

Evaluate the ethical and legal implications of your actions. Chapter Eight implied that many classroom management problems could be averted if teachers would carefully consider the ethical and legal implications of their actions. Indeed, much student defiance could be a direct result of their feeling that they are not being treated as they should be. In considering the problem of defiance, we recommend that you ask yourself:

1. Is the defiance a result of attempts to create unnecessary conformity? Do I give the students ample opportunity to question classroom goals?
2. Have the techniques (either positive or negative) I am using generated defiance? Would an alternative approach be just as acceptable without creating a similar problem?
3. Have I recognized the rights of the students? Are they being treated as I would treat adults? Have any basic privileges to which students are entitled by right been withheld?
4. Are some students being treated "more equally" than others?

Simulating Problem Situations

From the discussion of the preceding problem, you have probably surmised that no simple solution exists for managing classroom difficulties. Managing classroom problems effectively consists of considering all the factors that contribute to a problem,
and changing as many adverse factors as possible. Obviously, we
feel that changing personal attitudes, setting the stage for desirable behaviors, accenting appropriate behavior, developing alternative strategies for temporarily suppressing "serious" problems,
working with others, involving the students in self-management,
and adhering to the highest ethical and legal standards are key
factors to be considered in resolving problems. You would no
doubt agree that these are significant factors affecting classroom
behavior. But at this point you may be wondering which specific
techniques should be applied when several options are available
for remedying one of the factors. For instance, if immediate action is needed, which technique should be used: a soft reprimand,
time out, response cost, or overcorrection? The answer depends
on your setting, your students, and your own preferences. Some
school administrators may ask that certain techniques be avoided.
For example, some may object to experimenting with overcorrection. In such cases, you would probably prefer turning to other
options. The age of your students might preclude frequent use of
certain techniques. Frequent use of time out is less appropriate
with older than with younger students. Also, your experiences
with a student may reveal that one technique will work for him
while another technique does not. And you may prefer one
strategy over another. For instance, you may object to response
cost, but feel comfortable occasionally using a soft reprimand.
Probably, however, you will use most of the techniques with different students at different times. We think you ought to be familiar with as many alternatives for changing behavior as possible.
We also think you should be prepared to deal with a variety of
problems to prevent being caught without any idea of what is
happening when misbehavior occurs. For that reason, we are offering a number of simulated classroom problems to allow you
to practice working through different incidents before facing
them in class. Imagine yourself as the classroom teacher who must
deal with each of these common problems. Just as we did on the
problem of defiance, we suggest that you peruse Chapters Two
through Eight, selecting the techniques you believe most appro-

"Now, as we feed you these ideas, you play around with them, bringing your expertise and years of experience in the field to bear, then file them."

priate for each problem. Remember to: (1) Examine personal attitudes. (2) Set the stage for desirable behavior. (3) Accentuate appropriate behavior. (4) Consider developing alternative strategies for temporarily suppressing "seriously" disruptive behaviors. (5) Consider the need for working with others. (6) Involve the student. (7) Evaluate the ethical and legal implication of your actions.

1. One of your ninth graders, Jay, is absent from school more frequently than he is present. You are concerned about his truant behavior. What can you do to help keep Jay in school?

2. Christy is a very quiet, shy, and withdrawn fifth grader. You observe that she is a loner in class and that she does not approach other students. In addition, she is not approached by them. She seems to be an unhappy child. As her teacher, you are concerned about her inability to interact with her peers. What can you do to help her?

3. You notice that your eighth grade students are apathetic during history class. Very seldom do they comment and then only in response to your direct questions. You question the desirability of this situation. What can you do?

4. Scott tends to assume a threatening posture and is often verbally aggressive to other seventh graders. In particular, he engages in name-calling, and brags about beating up other boys if they bother him. How can this problem be resolved?

5. Andrea and Deborah are close friends. During class periods, they continually whisper and pass notes. Some of the other students complain that they cannot work because the whispering disturbs them. How can you deal with students who talk during class activities?

6. Several of your fourth grade boys are loud and boisterous during the lunch period. Their table manners are usually poor, but some days their manners are worse than others. For example, they throw bread and swap food, sometimes overloading their plates. The behavior of the students disrupts your own lunch periods. How can you create a calmer, more enjoyable lunch period for all?

7. Mary and Susan run to tell you that two of your fifth grade boys are fighting on the playground. This is not the first time that your boys have become involved in fights during the recess period. You do not wish to have the fights occur again. What can you do to deal immediately with the behavior at hand, and how can you prevent fights in the future?

8. Leroy appears to have good intentions about doing his school work. However, he seldom completes an assignment. You realize that something should be done to change his behavior. Analyze and provide suggestions for this common problem.

9. You enter your room on Friday to find desks overturned, walls decorated with writing, and papers strewn over the

floor. You are distressed at the wreckage, but must continue the day as usual. You feel, however, that something should be done about the vandalism problem. What are some things that you as a teacher might do?

10. Two of your tenth grade girls are consistently tardy to history class. They give one excuse and then another for being late. You want to give them the benefit of the doubt, but you are convinced that their excuses are invalid. What can you do to reduce their tardy behavior?

11. Your fourth grade students tend to run in the school halls unless directly supervised. In addition to being unsafe, this behavior is disruptive for other classes. You certainly do not wish to have it continue. What can you do to eliminate the problem of your students' running in the halls?

12. Several of your students are reported to create disturbances on the school bus. In particular, they push and shove and refuse to share seats with others. Is there anything you can do to reduce this behavior, even though you do not ride the bus?

13. Several students report that their school supplies and personal clothes have been "ripped off" at school. Problems with stealing appear to be increasing. What are some ways you might approach student theft?

14. It is becoming increasingly apparent that drugs and alcohol are problems for some of the students in your class. The problem obviously cannot be extinguished by ignoring it. What are some constructive ways of approaching it?

15. You have been given a teaching assignment as a twelfth grade English teacher in an inner city school. You find that students tend to group together with no interaction taking place among the various racial groups in your classroom. How would you approach this problem?

16. You have been asked to supervise a fifth period high school study hall class. You know that several big, boisterous boys have been assigned to this class. Therefore, you are concerned that you will be unable to maintain order and to deal with problems that may arise. However, you have no choice but to carry out this assignment. What are some ways that you might approach the study hall in order to minimize problems?

Concluding Remarks

Classroom management problems have always existed and, at least to some extent, always will. No one is suggesting that teachers can prevent every problem. Some problems are simply the result of normal interpersonal interactions. We are not sure life would be enjoyable if we never experienced any problems. Some of our most worthwhile achievements have come from gaining better understanding of ourselves as a result of working through a problem situation. Similarly, we have experienced much joy in helping others overcome difficulties and move toward greater self-control. However, it is one thing to face an occasional problem and another to live a life inundated with problems. Too many teachers tell us the latter situation characterizes life in today's classrooms. No one deserves such a fate. We think teachers can improve circumstances by becoming more aware of the techniques now available for improving most classrooms. But awareness alone will not make a good teacher. One must have the courage to apply what is known. There is a big difference between knowing and doing. We hope our book has helped increase your knowledge. If so, only the task of application remains. Only you can make the application.

INDEX